FRIENDSHIP CHRONICLES

Friendship Chronicles

Letters Between a Gay
and a Straight Man

by
Chris Hassett
and
Tom Owen-Towle

Illustrations by
Jim Bess *and* **Dan Lund**

Bald Eagle Mountain Press
San Diego, California

For information, write to: Bald Eagle Mountain Press, 9985 Huennekens Street, Suite B, San Diego, CA 92121.

FIRST EDITION

ISBN 0-9630636-1-8

Acknowledgments

We would like to thank Jim Bess for his beautifully natural and insightful drawings. Taken from his sketchbook, these drawings complement the personal and informal style of our letters better than any illustrations we might have commissioned. Jim's painting on the cover—more typical of his studio work—demonstrates his talents as a strong colorist.

Several drawings are by Dan Lund whose early years in the beautiful Northwest helped shape his innate drawing skills. Although his career was cut short by AIDS at age 37, his work as an art educator, illustrator, graphic artist, and art naturalist continues to delight and inspire a multitude of friends, students, and family.

We especially want to thank our friend Mark Belletini for his thoughtful editing and for his passionate encouragement of this project. His considerable talents in arts and letters and in all endeavors human inspire us both. We dedicate this book perhaps not directly to Mark but rather to his capacity for friendship which sets a lofty though reachable standard for all of us who strive to live with an open heart.

Finally, Tom and I would like to thank our significant others— Carolyn and Mitch, respectively—for their well-contained curiosity and understanding as we pursued this project. In this book which honors friendship, we can both express genuine gratitude for the friendships embodied in our primary partnerships.

Contents

List of Illustrations

Introduction

We have chosen to introduce this book by each writing a letter to you, the reader. Tom first, and then Chris.

Dear Reader,

You are going to know plenty about me and Chris before you exit the final door of this book, but some comments, at the outset, about my personal life might provide a helpful context. I am a 52-year-old citizen of the universe who has been married twice, currently for the past twenty years; the father of four grown children; a parish minister since 1967, who has been enmeshed equally in spiritual disciplines and social causes. I have been exploring issues of men's intimacy since 1972 and began gay-straight dialogues a few years later being prodded by a gay activist in my Iowa congregation. Since coming to San Diego in 1978, my wife, Carolyn, and I as co-ministers have been ongoingly committed to creating a genuinely Welcoming Congregation for persons of variant sexual orientations. While falling short of our aspirations, we have remained steadfast on that course.

Chris Hassett and I met back in 1981 during one of our worship services where I was liturgist and he was soloist. Our friendship has evolved ever since, and this book, while not doing full justice to the twists and turns of our bond, is partial fruition of our joyful communion.

Chris and I have found that bridging the sexual orientation gulf is one of our toughest socio-ethical challenges in American culture because of the bedrock insecurity, angst, and self-doubt involved. We males are more uptight about sexual identity than anything imaginable, even our own mortality. Issues of erotic preference cause us to squirm, become defensive and rigid, often lash out belligerently. Conversely, when we men—gays, straights, and bisexuals—risk moving from closets to closeness, speaking our deepest truths, venturing beneath surfaces, beyond expectations, and beside prejudices, the results are frequently most gratifying indeed. That has certainly proven true for the two of us.

Friendship between men, in an increasingly impersonal, macho, lonely, even violent culture, is no longer a luxury but a necessity. We males have contributed to a patriarchal system which dehumanizes us all. We must unlearn that training, starting here, starting now. However, fostering male friendships will require all the creativity and integrity we men can muster, for we dwell in a society which is both homophobic and philiaphobic. This double whammy renders male intimacy a rare accomplishment.

C.S. Lewis recalls that "to the ancients, friendship seemed the happiest and most fully human of all loves." It seemed purer and more substantial than romance. Friendship was considered the crucial means by which humans achieved our highest cultural values. We simply could not develop the good society alone. We needed holy, intimate bonds of affection. We coveted friends. Yet friendship, since the Industrial Revolution, became progressively difficult to sustain, especially between men. Slowly but surely, it fell out of favor. It pretty much disappeared from the relational landscape.

So, one of the major movements of the closing moments of the 20th century is the re-establishment of male community. The essential ingredient missing in men's lives has been other men. We are now eagerly addressing that absence by occasioning opportunities for comradeship and conversation with our brothers. Men are ritualizing our brothering ties with support groups, retreats, discussions, and ceremonies conducted in a serious yet playful manner.

We men are learning that healthy, animated friendships with other men enhance rather than jeopardize our bonds with women and children. Everyone in the male universe benefits when our brothering hungers are genuinely met. As Perry Garfinkel astutely notes: "How can we work it out with the opposite sex until we've worked it out with our own?" We can't.

Male friendships won't all resemble Chris and Tom. We are not prescribing what close male bonds must entail, but we are promoting the fundamental importance of male–male intimacy. Furthermore, as the situation presents itself, we are encouraging men to grow affectional companionship across sexual orientation lines. Let it also be acknowledged from the start that our growing friendship is not all sweetness and ease. There are sizeable holes and fences in our brothering quest. Ours is a sturdy yet fragile web of entangled vines. Unfinished. Ever evolving.

We are both, by the way, partial to the term "friends." We use other synonyms periodically, but our preference is clear. Why? Well, we don't choose to be partners: legal, erotic, or otherwise. We weren't childhood chums, starting instead as adult acquaintances. We are more than companions, who, after all, can be hired. Soulmates sound too ethereal. So just call us friends, nothing more and nothing less.

Even though we live in the same town, letters have furnished the most natural yet evocative medium to convey what lies in our hearts and spins through our minds. We have found letter–writing to be a remarkably intimate exercise. Each of us, to be sure, has a distinctive writing style and singular way of divulging our interiors. I know that I am predisposed to philosophical excursions; I only hope that my reflective jaunts prove relevant, even engaging. My goal remains to be personal not private in my self-disclosures. Some of my inner material is simply too intimate to share. Certain stories, which implicate others including loved ones, are best kept confidential. I learned years back that truth-telling is an instrumental value not a terminal one; our revelations, to be useful not merely titillating, must try to serve larger, redemptive purposes. With that aspiration in mind, I have tried to express myself with personal–philosophical integrity in this volume of letters.

One more thing. Our culture prefers instancy rather than constancy—quick results and rapid relationships. But if Chris and I have learned anything, it is that friendship, the real article, requires both rigorous cultivation and abundant time. Sam Keen concurs: "Friendship thrives only in slow time. . . . the cadence of friendship is measured in decade-long rhythms."

So it does. Our friendship is relatively young, rounding into its fourteenth year. We have shared meals, run together, unnerved one another, joked around, sung in a quartet, been fully present for the other during various life-passages of anguish and celebration. But we have "miles and miles to go before we sleep," before one of us ceases to breathe. And, even then, after death, our friendship will ripple on.

So, welcome, readers, to our ordinary yet revolutionary friendship!

With anticipation,
Tom

Dear Reader,

Our friendship consists of two stories, not a single composite story. There are two voices present in this book, mine and Tom's. Each voice develops many tones. The voices alternate. One voice may hold forth for a while and then pause, sometimes inviting a response from the other. Silence facilitates the exchange of human sounds just as the space between dancers shapes movement. So it is with friendship. Part chatter, part dance. All human.

I feel that men have a knack for friendship yet male friendships seldom reach full bloom. Has our innate talent been overtaken by power maneuvers, pride, and other learned dynamics? Has our talent for friendship been subverted? Too often we let our friendships stray into ritual or ennui—constrained by circumstance, bent by social pressures, and distorted by our own insecurities.

Tom and I embarked on this shared enterprise as a means of discovering who we are to each other and, through reflection, who we might be to ourselves. Through our letters, Tom and I have explored not only *our* friendship but friendship in general. We have tried to keep the letters as fresh as they were when we first wrote them and first read them. We have taken the opportunity to revise here and there, primarily to enhance communication with a larger audience. Letters originally written to a single, good friend have been made accessible to readers who don't know us. At least, not yet.

From the beginning, we endeavored to keep our letters focused on honest dialog and personal friendship. Admittedly, we considered publishing our letters early on. If you find our stories less remarkable than you'd expect to find in a book, we hope that their freshness and sense of discovery make up for that shortfall. Our friendship began long before this book was conceived and continues beyond these pages. But, for a period of time, these letters parallel our friendship, make comments on our friendship, and serve as a partial chronicle of our friendship. Lives of course remain largely unrecorded.

We know that our friendship is just one of countless friendships in this world. Consider however that friendships are the building blocks for social interaction and for civilization and this two-man case study quickly takes on more noble dimensions. Thankfully we didn't consider such a grand purpose at the outset. Though we hope our letters affirm and model a robust friendship, we certainly do not hold ours up as the ultimate friendship. Nor have we tried to write a "How to" book on friendship. And we hope we haven't air-brushed our flaws away or sanitized our spirits.

What rests in your hands is an honest written account of friendship. A book of letters between two men. One gay. One straight. Friends. Contemporaries. Chosen brothers.

Friendship has both the gentleness of touch and the power of revolution in its quiver. Tom and I have brought these arrows and many more onto our bows and taken careful aim. We intend to be true. To person and to process.

Tom's letters were originally done on a typewriter. Mine were either handwritten or composed on a computer. Many were first entered into my journal with a "Dear Tom" at the front. Most likely, Tom sat at a desk to compose his letters; my letters found life in a wide variety of situations—offices, coffee houses, parks, buses, and trains—just about anywhere.

Because Tom and I alternate as authors, we wondered how we might visually cue the reader as to who was speaking. Should we use different type styles, we wondered? We even considered presenting the letters in their original form. Neither idea lasted very long. We've settled on a traditional presentation and hope you find our voices distinct without the prompting.

We have not presented the letters in strict chronology. Tom and I have grouped the letters to reflect the phases and themes of a growing friendship. Also, in telling our stories, we sometimes have changed names and details. Though we are committed to revealing our truths, others need to be protected from having that decision made for them.

Diversity is the rule when surveying human relationships;

perhaps the activities of friendship catch us in our most naturally human state—laughing, telling stories, complaining, whispering, gossiping, and when the spirit moves us, writing letters.

Wishing you happy letters. And we might add, we welcome yours.

Sincerely,
Chris

Off and Writing

Bold acts of consciousness are, I think, the true basis for an art of friendship these days. No gimmicks will work. The acts of friendship we need are inner acts, acts of depth of the heart, of self-searching, and of decision.

Stuart Miller

Tom and I share many experiences in life—we run together, we both love music and sometimes sing together, we enjoy writing and sharing letters, and we belong to the same church community.

Because our lives blend in so many ways, different activities are just different aspects of our shared friendship. These various activities overlap and commingle. During our runs, for instance, I have been known to limn a new melody and Tom has defined sermon topics. Sometimes when we rehearse our singing, we have laughed uproariously and, on other musical occasions, have been moved spiritually.

Writing has allowed us deliberate exploration of our experiences as friends and has sharpened our senses for continuing adventures. In this first set of letters, we write about some of the activities we share.

A running conversation

Dear Chris,

One of the customary and critical appointments on my calendar has been our five-mile run through Balboa Park, beginning at 6:45 on Tuesday mornings. Our course is filled with hills, valleys, and clusters of lush groves, sprinkled with spectacular architectural sites and cultural landmarks, and graced with animal sounds emanating from our world-famous zoo. There are few people, cars, or annoyances.

Ours is a *running* conversation for two reasons. We *jog* at a mutually selected clip, and it is an *ongoing* engagement, one that is strictly honored unless either of us is ill or out of town. I count on us running long and far into our tomorrows.

It's a conversation, because we discuss as we run. Talking while running gives us rare, focused, one-on-one time as well as distracting us from the normal aches and strains our bodies incur. Running together is a lovely, healthy way to wake up our bodies and minds simultaneously.

After catching up on each other's lives, we flow into deeper stuff. Perhaps the chemical changes created by rigorous physical exercise open us for spiritual exploration? Or is it the tranquillity and beauty of the journey? Or both? Whatever. Our conversation topics range from prayer to rallies, from stress to romance.

I fondly recall the first 10K we ran together. Our plan was to race together for the entire route, but we jousted at the outset. "Chris, if you want to run faster, just go ahead." "Tom, I don't know what I'm up for today. I think you're in better shape."

Well, we stayed close throughout, sprinting the final 100 yards alongside each other, hands clutched and arms raised together as we broke the tape. It was exhilarating, cementing.

Running conversations are a sacred place reserved for our man-to-man sharing and caring.

Your friend,
Tom

"Will the calendulas still be there?"

Dear Tom,

Your letter made it clear to me that our running together on Tuesday mornings is an experience that is part shared and part isolated—both communal and personal. I can affirm much of what you said and yet, as I look more closely at our running experiences, I seem to uncover some of the hidden aspects as well.

First of all, I've always loved the idea of waking up early and starting the day with the dawn. Having one's body and mind attuned to the primal dance of earth and sun almost seems a prerequisite for accomplishing any important task. I believe that the colors of the eastern sky just before sunrise must inspire all that breathes on this Earth. Our works, dreams, and loves are at best faint echoes of this daily glory.

However, when morning hits, it's not that way with me. I cling to my bed. Whether the sheets are cold or warm, they are my only comfort. There may be noise outside, my pillow will block it out. There may be fantastic smells from the kitchen, I'll have cereal later. Understand, Tom, that when we run on Tuesday mornings at 6:45 am, my day begins with a few moments of agony. On Tuesday mornings, my willpower, assigned with the unenviable task of getting my ass out of bed, gets the first workout.

My body wakes up gradually. I reach for my glasses first thing—a special register of memory unfailingly recalls where I left them the night before. I roll, swivel, and get out of bed. The morning cold, once I've left the bed, doesn't affect me. Skin that a few moments ago had to be swathed in flannel now breaks the morning chill without complaints. My feet shuffle—mainly a habit from old running injuries. Amazingly, runners collect a lot of small pains and just as many small adjustments to minimize them.

My running gear is always easy to find. I only have a few shorts—my favorites being a pair of black, cotton gym shorts I bought at a garage sale for 50¢. I have a million t-shirts—something else runners collect. Anyway I get myself assembled and head off to our rendezvous at the park. Driving to the park I notice that I'm a few minutes late. You must notice it too but you never mention it. I used to flash my lights when I'd see you waiting but now, with one headlight out, I'm embarrassed. Why don't I fix that? Why don't I get up a little earlier? So many recriminations.

Greetings are quiet but you always smile. We shake out the kinks and start taking easy steps on the sidewalk. At first, words come out awkwardly, like our body movements. We always comment on the day's chief attribute—other than *early*, that is. Whether it's warm, cold, wet, dry, or pleasant. Single words usually suffice for now though I suspect you are ready for more advanced communication. We shuffle along Upas Street toward the canyon and begin to string words together, slowly rolling out an overview of the week. Topics may be nominated for discussion but there's no strong need at this point to lock in on any one item. Anything notable about the morning itself—grass, eucalyptus, or sidewalk—still takes precedence. The tangible is so much easier to deal with.

If we're lucky, we're limber enough for the first downhill just a few hundred yards into the run. The footing is good as we follow a cement sidewalk down to a foot bridge. The smell of exhaust, especially on cold days, reminds me of visiting Kansas City as a boy when I was fascinated by the roar and smell of diesel buses. We pass through a cold, low spot and then cross the bridge with vine-covered fences that shield us from the sight of traffic, even though its sound and stink have already made their impressions.

We face our first uphill and climb an asphalt path out of the canyon. Dogs run along the fences and voice their combined greetings and warnings as we pass by. After a few hundred yards of ascent, we strain for breath and rhythm. Sometimes I become the coach about halfway up. "Swing those arms. Work that hill," I might intone, subconsciously giving into my years as a swim coach. And as we get to the top, we always have a comment.

"Whew, that hill was tough today!" one of us might exclaim. Or "I felt that!"

Then we stretch out along the other side of Upas. At this point, we finally become running partners—the hill has knocked the last bit of grogginess out of me and put both of us through our first test. Now, on the flat, we recover—breaking a sweat and fully alive. We usually start responding to each other better and engage in our first conversation about now. As we turn in front of the school at Upas and Park, we pass a warm spot sheltered by the building and warmed by the sun now appearing in a beautiful eastern sky. I'd run in circles there for awhile if I had *my* way. But *our* way leads on.

We lope along through the zoo parking lot. With the hill behind us and our bodies warmed by the sun, we broaden our conversation and tackle bigger topics, larger perspectives. We supply each other with segués, invite responses—almost like we needed to reaffirm the familiar while we look for differences. In the zoo parking lot, the world comes into focus.

By the time we reach the Spanish Village, a group of buildings that house small art studios, my bladder usually pleads for release so I take a quick detour. I rejoin you around the Museum of Natural History. My friend Rathbun told me that the museum looked to him like frozen organ music. I never run past it without thinking of that description and nodding in agreement.

We lope across the plaza, past the fountain, and down a cement path into another canyon. Our stride is easier, our muscles and joints looser, so we give into the hill with more smoothness. Our conversation deepens and we talk of family issues, personal topics: children, parents, lovers. Striding across the short flat stretch at the bottom of the canyon, we accelerate our sharing, getting it all out before we face the steep climb up the far side of the canyon. We begin the steep road together. We share a determination to overcome the hill almost as a statement of faith that we can overcome whatever personal issues we have just raised. On some days, one of us pumps ahead, maybe feeling the greater need to solve a particular problem.

We slow at the top and run in place to get our wind back as we wait for a break in the traffic to cross the road. We resume our conversation quickly as though we need to let our tongues catch up with our minds' activities during that last climb. We sweep around the back side of the Starlight Bowl and the Aerospace Museum and are treated to a great view of downtown. About now, some of our first summation statements come. What might have been delivered as observations earlier in our run are now wrapped in brightly feathered opinions and projected strongly into the morning air. Through the museum parking lot and international village, across the wooden bridge that looks down into a tropical grotto, our heavy steps pounding out a primitive tattoo. Then we venture into my favorite park venu, Alcazar Gardens. I love this scene whether I find flowers, young plants, or just freshly prepared soil. "Will the calendulas still be there?" "Oh, they've been replaced by zinnias." "When will they plant the dahlias?" A few steps around the raised beds, the tiled fountain, and then down the steps and out of the gardens.

It's all effortless now—heart, lungs, and muscles have found their rhythm and propel us across the bridge as we soar hundreds of feet over the downtown commuters in their earthbound cars. We pivot off the sidewalk and onto a series of grass and dirt paths that loop gracefully alongside the park boulevard.

I remember turning down a shaded path where the ground is usually moist and dark and being ambushed one morning by an exposed root that my feet didn't quite clear. As I tripped, my upper body lurched forward, my pitch made worse by the downhill grade. My legs, instantaneously lightened by a gush of adrenaline, raced to get back under my flailing arms and torso. Luckily, about where the ground begins to flatten again, I managed to stabilize in an upright position and turned to match your shocked gaze with my own. With my heart still pounding, I said, "You know, I've always had a gift for recovery." We bounced back and forth talking about the incident and managed to expand the ten-second episode into about ten minutes. And here I sit, expanding it again.

FRIENDSHIP CHRONICLES

Then we run up Sixth Avenue and approach the car. You break off to begin your day and I am grateful to feel so alive. To have accomplished a 5-mile run by 7:30 in the morning gives me a tremendous feeling of pride and I'm ready for the day.

I also feel that I've had a wonderful run with you, my buddy Tom; the experience is part shared and part private. Our runs—the sweat, the strain, the exhilaration, the conversation, and the recoveries—are an important part of our busy lives.

There are mornings when our running experience reveals the maps of our inner lives. On others, our newsy conversation helps us establish our places in the world. And on *some* mornings, our run through the park *is* our journey. It's great to navigate this life alongside one another.

Love,
Chris

Singing

> God respects us when we work, but loves us when
> we sing.
>
> Rabindranath Tagore

Dear Chris,

One of your primary life struggles, it appears, my friend, is not whether work is more important than singing but how you might meld them in a unified vocation.

You have been singing since you were four. Your family is a batch of unrepentant crooners who might aptly be called the von Hassett singers. You sang during your teen years, then did your share of folk festivals and night club gigs in college and early adulthood. But always on the side.

Now, after multiple overwhelmingly successful "Friends and Lovers" concerts for greater San Diego to raise funds in the struggle against AIDS, you are expanding your horizons. Who knows what will transpire with your singing future? All I know, Chris, is that your vocal gifts are exceptional. I know it. Others know it. You know it.

You exude range, interpretive power, and soul. You reach deep down inside your spacious spirit, shape exquisite vocal creations, then deliver them to us. Goosebumps, tears, and smiles are constant companions whenever I hear you sing. As Holly Near said to Ronnie Gilbert: "Singing with you is the best thing that can happen to me, my friend." I know whereof she speaks.

The first time we met was when you sang an energetic, poignant Pat Benatar song to underscore Carolyn's Sunday sermon on "Child Abuse." Afterwards, we both remarked: "We've got to get to know that guy better, maybe even sing with him someday." Thus began our "TOO FAB Four" vocal group consisting of you and Mary, Carolyn and me.

Our musical life has been immensely satisfying to me. Eating together, sharing our personal highs and lows, rehearsing songs, then performing in modest concerts. All four of us, as you say, are "hopelessly pop," specializing in melodic ballads from recent decades.

Remember a year or so ago, Chris, when, dressed in 1950's garb, we sang "Sugartime," "Dream," and "Don't It Make Your Brown Eyes Blue" at a local extravaganza, then went dancing at Corvette's Diner afterward. What a grand, glorious night was had by all!

I also cherish the several times we have sung "That's What Friends Are For." Its affecting refrain, "through good times and bad times, I'll be on your side forever more, that's what friends are for . . . " expresses the sentiment of our fierce, unbreakable bond.

Carl Sandburg once wrote to Archibald MacLeish saying: "My word to you: go on singing and dreaming." MacLeish was a poet who serenaded with his pen. You are also a wordsmith, but quintessentially a vocalist, the finest I've ever had the privilege of knowing, hearing up close, harmonizing with.

And I say, keep on singing and dreaming, Chris, from the inner recesses of your soul.

Your friend,
Tom

P.S. You've already sung "What A Wonderful World" at the memorial services of both my father-in-law and sister-in-law, Millard and Lee. At my service, please sing "Vincent," "The Rose," "Memory," and any others you and Carolyn might select, knowing well that whatever you choose to sing will assuredly soothe my soul in its final resting place.

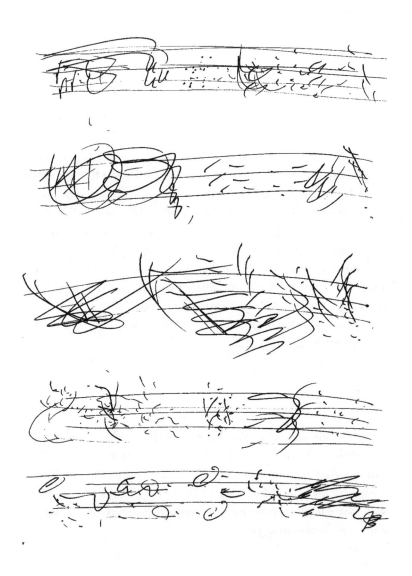

FRIENDSHIP CHRONICLES

Goose bumps

Dear Tom,

I sang at church this morning. At First Unitarian Church. My church. Our church. As always, it was a positive experience for me and (if my fans can be given any credibility) a good experience for the crowd as well. Reading your letter about our singing has put me in an historical mood and thought I'd share some musings with you.

As you mentioned, about ten years ago I was asked to sing a song about child abuse for a Sunday service. "Hell Is for Children," by Pat Benatar, is a poignant song that builds to a hard driving finish. I accompanied myself on the guitar—something I never do in public these days. I've found too many *good* instrumentalists so I no longer indulge in that folly. Anyway, I had sung that same song on a TV show some weeks earlier. Someone in the congregation had heard me and thought it would be a good addition to Carolyn's sermon.

All this "Someone heard . . . someone thought . . . and maybe . . . could you? . . . " It amazes me how many profound connections in our lives start off so tenuously. Sharing my music both in our church and with the larger community has become one of my richest and most gratifying endeavors. Hard to believe that something so strong required so little nurturing and planning at the outset. Once the connection was established, however, vigorous nurturing prevailed all around. So, here I am.

Had I already met Carolyn? Yes. At another time, she had appeared on the TV show and we had a short but animated conversation in the hallway about our shared faith. Shortly after that, I began attending the church—somewhat fitfully but always with a healthy mix of curiosity and the hope that I would find a spiritual home there. My hopes have been fulfilled.

I also met Mary Barranger that day. Thank God Mary came up after the service and gave me her card, suggesting we get together soon to play some music. Little did I know what a musical treasure I had conversed with so nonchalantly on the patio after church that morning. After many concerts and countless songs performed at weddings, memorial services, birthdays, cabaret nights, and just about any other excuse for music, Mary and I still revel in our musical partnership.

We have our own personal styles, our own musical directions—she is principal pianist for the San Diego Symphony and, as you pointed out, I am hopelessly pop—our own personal visions for artistic expression, and our own busy lives—sometimes making collaboration more a matter of logistics than music. My musical partnership with Mary has been a breakthrough life experience for me. And the friendship, too. I'm almost overwhelmed as I sit here and, in my mind, begin to sift through the music notebooks, rehearsal notes, schedules, concert programs, cassette labels, pictures, and thank you cards that line my decade of musical memories with Mary.

And you and Carolyn are a big part of those memories. A golden thread of music weaves in and out of our times together. Life, not just lives, has brought us together on so many occasions. We've shared tears, laughs, and big, warm smiles. And yes, prominent among my musical memories are the times we performed as a quartet—the TOO FAB Four. I've always laughed that we have one of the few names that requires an explanation. TOO FAB is an acronym for "three out of four ain't bad" which seemed to describe the prevailing dynamic at our rehearsals—we seldom had a consensus so three out of four was the next best thing.

Even better than the memories is knowing we all have the desire and the craziness to do it again and again. Can life really be this abundant, I sometimes ask myself?

Could you or I turn off these goose bumps right now even if we wanted to? I don't think so.

Enough for now. Here's to wonderful memories . . . that reach far into the future. And here's looking at you, kid.

Love,
Chris

Families

Family means love.

John Lennon

Dear Chris,

I am thankful this day for our multiple families.

For my nuclear family—my wife whom you respect and enjoy, my four children whom you've met and connected with at varying levels. Now that Erin is considering your college alma mater as her own, our family grows more familiar.

I remember your brother Jeff's wedding, at which you blended two songs from yesteryear and now: "How Deep is the Ocean" and "Longer." What made the occasion extraordinarily rich for our two clans was the fact that the couple who introduced my parents to one another back in 1932 are the grandparents of the woman whom your brother married. Again, Chris, you and I are linked, by family lines this time.

I think of your wonderful parents, Doris and Frank, with whom we have shared unforgettable musical events and religious ceremonies. They light up the room whenever they enter it.

Then your pilgrimage to see Carolyn's folks in Northern California meant a lot to us. We prepared the way for your visit by playing for them a tape of your songs. There is nothing more gratifying in life than to introduce friends to friends, loved ones to loved ones. We did just that during our shared weekend in Anchor Bay. We also hiked out on the promontory, visited galleries, and basked in the grandeur of this Golden State that we all cherish as natives.

Then there is the gay–lesbian–bisexual family in our San Diego environs, before whom we have sung at fund-raisers and political events, a family into which you have eased and welcomed us foreigners.

Finally, our church family of sisters and brothers, gays, straights and bisexuals, young and old, persons of different racial backgrounds and theological bents melding together in a single community of integrity and acceptance. . . a community that upholds us in our despair, jolts us in our apathy, rejoices with us during our triumphs.

We are well–familied!

Your friend,
Tom

Our _other_ families

Dear Tom,

I found myself nodding in agreement as I read your letter about families. I'm indeed fortunate to have the love and support of my Mom and Dad and of my four brothers and their families. What I also feel, especially as a gay man, is the absolute importance of my _other_ families—my _chosen families_—made up of friends, acquaintances, colleagues, and other kindred spirits. Connections between non–blood-related people are truly the bonds that heal the world. Reaching _across_ families and into the hearts of _distant_ cousins builds an enduring community.

I love many members of our church precisely because they are different from my usual group of buddies. I think of the older women whose hearts seem to embrace the whole world, whose hands have raised families, and whose abundant wisdom rests quietly behind soft, knowing eyes. It's hard not to be romantic in my appreciation for these women.

I think of the young mamas and papas, whose fertile relationships tug at my heart and who bring a prayer to my lips for the important work they undertake. I watch young couples bring children into the world, guide them through startling growth, and then send them out into the world. I marvel at people with apparent disabilities but whose stride never falters and others who struggle purposefully to erase emotional scars. I think of men and women who confront their own prejudices. I witness a community of people who live life fully, who accept who they are, and reach toward who they can be.

Such bravery. Living among giants, I sometimes feel like one myself because, after all, they have let me into their castle. When I am stricken by pettiness, jealousy, and insecurity, I remind myself of the heroic work that simply living can be. And then I embrace my family and myself once again. Here's a hug for you, Tom.

Love, Chris

The dancers

. . . the dancers are free, barely touching as they pass yet partners in the same pattern.

Anne Morrow Lindbergh

Dear Chris,

Every Summer, from our adventures of renewal, Carolyn and I find some fresh treasure to lug homeward and grace our lives. This last year we returned with a bronze sculpture, crafted by a Northern California artist-friend, Robert Holmes, entitled "The Dancers." You have seen it nestled majestically in our living room corner.

We fell in love with "The Dancers" because it is a striking visual dialogue between two creations, like our friendship—cool and precise, yet warm and humane; spiritual as well as sensual. In its semi-abstract form it reminds us that friendship bridges the real and imaginary, the practical and visionary realms.

"The Dancers" reminds us of the male-female connections as well as the male-male and female-female ties in our lives. I perceive an expressed parity here. Who is leading, who is following in the dance called friendship? I say both. So does the sculpture. For in a good dance you don't worry unduly about leading and following; what matters is that the swirl goes on.

The sculpture reminds us of the tension, the pull, the stretch necessary in any creative dance. As poet Marge Piercy writes, "loving leaves stretch marks."

Note that the dancers are neither clinging to one another nor bounding unfettered. They are neither leaning upon nor propped up by the other. They stand tall, separate, with clasped hands, swaying. I think of us, Chris. Ours is an easy exchange, like our weekly runs in the park. We lope along, companionably, neither pressuring nor clinging. We can go long periods without saying much of anything. I never feel claustrophobic around you. I don't have to tell, do, be all. My presence is enough. The strength of each of us flows into the other. Yes, we are dancers—free, barely touching as we pass, yet partners in the same pattern.

"The Dancers" reminds us that friendship never ossifies but keeps whirling. This sculpture exudes movement and so do we. It reminds us that life as a dance is fun, abundant with mirth and frolicking. Friendship is a challenge but neither a drab struggle nor a bitter battle. As Conrad Hyers writes: "Life is a contest more than a conflict, a play of forces, a sporting proposition, an interplay of opposites, a cosmic dance . . . "

The sculpture dares us to be foolish, jitterbug, reel, and waltz all our days. Our friendship doesn't need to freeze into one cadence or step. Each dance is ours to shape as we choose.

"The Dancers" reminds us with its openness between the figures, that the spaces between friends are as shapely and significant as any intertwining embrace. As Kahlil Gibran states: "Let there be spaces in our togetherness, and let the winds of heaven dance between us . . . "

"The Dancers" reminds us that cut off from another's touch and grip, we tumble and crash to the ground, yet with the light, firm hold of comrades we dance adventurously and gracefully into myriad tomorrows.

Finally, Chris, "The Dancers" reminds us, with its outstretched arms, to welcome the outsider into our personal space. There is a time and place to dance alone with our special friend, and there is also a season for the circle dance. Holding on to the familiar friend with one hand, we reach out with the other hand for a newcomer so that our dancing stays varied, inclusive, fresh.

Chris, may our friendship dance long and lovingly into seasons beyond counting.

Your friend,
Tom

Edge–Dwellers

> It is not given us to live lives of undisrupted calm, boredom, and mediocrity. It is given us to be edge-dwellers.
>
> Jay Deacon

I don't think it's presumptuous to say that Chris and I, in our evolving friendship, are living on the edge.

Indeed, I am writing this from a dwelling in Northern California located on cliffs overlooking the Pacific Ocean. To get here one swivels back and forth on a narrow road perched precariously above that magnificent body of water. One false move, and you plummet to sure death.

Along with countless others, we are enmeshed in the revolutionary struggle of gay and lesbian rights plus gay–straight friendship for the duration of our earthly existence. We are lifers. We will not only overstep socially respectable boundaries along the way but extend the very boundaries themselves.

Our friendship is personally enriching for the two of us, but it signifies more. It is another example of humans huddling together to combat prejudice, build trust, raise hell, prove that strangeness of identity is holy, to be honored, and need never degenerate into estrangement.

Here on the edge of danger and possibility I am reminded of Guilliamne Appolinaire's empowering invitation to the frightened among us: "Come, my friends, come closer to the edge." And we cry out: "No, no, we can't come closer; we will fall into the canyon below. We will die." The exhortation continues: "Come, my friends, come closer."

Finally, some of the brave ones in our human clan creep closer to the edge of the cliff. Then soar.

In this set of letters, Chris and I probe more. Some letters betray our proximity to the edge. And others find us stewing in our "undisrupted calm." The "push and pull" of our friendship rears its mischievous head and I can see, upon rereading these letters, the rich and subtle ways we shape and influence each other's life.

New Year's Day

Dear Tom,

Tom, my thoughts have often been with you and Carolyn since I heard your father died on Christmas Eve. Now on New Year's Day, I'm moved to write you a note of sympathy and friendship.

Our friendship grows when we share our feelings and insights—the invisible cornerstones of our lives. My friendship with you, Tom, enhances my sense of belonging. It enables me to develop and express my caring side and our friendship is a precious source of laughter, love and all that is good. Collectively, the friendships I have in this world challenge me to embrace the utter mystery of life and death. In the relative shelter of friendship, I can grapple with the boundary of my skin. Of my soul.

Losing your father is an event of great sadness for your family and for everyone who loves you. We are all affected. I experience echoes of grief for the loved ones I have lost and shake with the fear of losing others I still hold close.

The pain of loss can sometimes be so great that I have become desperate to escape it. I've tried to reason it away, but have found little consolation in wrapping up in some rational assessment of it all—an ill-fitting mantle if there ever was one. Take this off-the-rack example: our feelings of loss are born of an inability to accept that we never really possessed anything anyway.

"Ouch!" you cry. "Got something a little more comfortable?" These garments may keep out the wind but they do nothing to take away the inner chill. Each cloak comes with its own dagger. In times of grief, there are truly lessons to be learned but . . . these lessons? Now?

When I have tried to replace the loss, nothing else really seems the right shape or size for that hole within me. Eventually, through a mysterious and flawed process that defies understanding, I may be lucky enough to accept the loss and once again turn my attentions to the life that surrounds me. As I know you have experienced, in accepting loss we can discover an increased capacity for giving and accepting love.

So there it is—the approach to loss as I understand it.

Another thought that fights within me for expression revolves around the perplexing yet natural event of a son losing a father. It must seem that you lose a part of yourself. Am I right, Tom? Or does it seem that you suddenly must take on what your father can no longer carry? Does his departure mean that—in the continuing world—there is now a little less bone and a little less muscle to move this grand enterprise of "life" forward?

Life. Don't push me for a definition here! Though I do have this suddenly appearing metaphor of a ship's cargo. When something is removed from the ship's hold, the crew needs to redistribute the weight a little—that is, trim the boat. And so we adjust—ourselves, our responsibilities, our values, our world. Change, brought on by the loss, ripples and rumbles through our fragile craft. The result may eventually be a more seaworthy vessel. Ideally, crew and passengers are empowered as well. The ship affirms its course. Living muscle and strong bone honor the loss by renewing their purpose.

A final thought, which in retrospect should have been my first, requires a simpler voice. I love you both. I care about you a lot. I think of you often. I feel so lucky to be aboard this fragile craft with you. May we always be guided by love and may there always be muscle and bone to propel us.

Love,
Chris

Thank you

Dear Chris,

Months later, I am still grieving my father's death. I remain challenged by his example, however convoluted and imperfect, of a good, generous man. Although you met my Dad briefly at your brother's wedding, Chris, I have need to tell you more about this first and special man in my life—personal things about his living and dying. I believe that sharing a portion of the story of my father whom I cherish, with my friend whom I cherish, will prove both cathartic and bonding in mysterious and wondrous ways. I am unspeakably grateful that our exchanging of letters grants me this opportunity. Thank you.

My Mom keeps repeating, "Harold was a good man, the best I ever knew." Now, Dad wasn't a great man by the measurable standards of fame, stature, or success. No, his unadorned mission on earth was simply to be a good person, good as in gentle and generous, without guile, brimming with integrity. A good husband, a good father, a good grandfather, a good musician, a good insurance counselor, a good servant to the larger community—in short, a good man. The only way my Dad knew how to spell God was with two O's.

His health started to plummet in November, and he left us on Christmas Eve. He died quickly and peacefully of a pulmonary embolism. It's remarkable to me that he kept on selling insurance, at the age of nearly 82, up until his trip to the hospital from which he never returned. Dad remained cogent and communicative up to his last day. My mother, brother, and I all got to speak our farewells, sum up our time together, and offer ample love. There was nothing that we said at the end that we hadn't shared in one version or another earlier along life's path.

Dad was the consummate provider, Chris. He spent his adult life essentially taking care of his family, then others. During the last several months he even made special, detailed lists of financial data so that when he died Mom would be secure. This was without any of us knowing or talking about it. I found his scribbled notes and figures shortly after he died.

Dad's heart, lungs, and will finally just let go—as if he were saying: "I'm at peace with my life. I have no major regrets. My love is known and shared. My soulmate, playmate, helpmate, Mary, is taken care of. My job is done. There is nothing really left for me to be or do. Farewell." So he let go and moved on.

My father took such consistently generous care of his family that after his passing into the final silence, I still periodically wail out, "But who will take care of my brother Phil and me now, who will bring care packages to us, who will handle our insurance policies, who will allow us to be little boys, what will happen to us now as sons?" Irrational or not, that's how I felt deep-down.

I knew Dad might go any day when he first came out of surgery, but when Mom called me on Christmas Eve I was as stunned as if hit by a sledgehammer. Viscerally, I didn't want to believe that Dad had really died. After all, aren't parents indestructible, immortal, always there when you need them? I know it doesn't make any sense, Chris, but my primitive, inconsolable need remains to have one or both of my parents there when I close out my life, just as they were there when first I entered it.

My Dad had the blessed benefit of a full life, but whether we die at eighteen, three months, 42 or 100 years old, to die is to die. Our death is our death, and we only have one of them. And last Christmas Eve was my father's death. It was no less significant because he was an old man. It was his death, the only one he will ever have. He was the only father I will ever have.

There is an evocative Navaho phrase which resounds in my mind: "My father died—he left me the earth." That's how I feel now that Dad is gone. I have to contend with the entire earth. I know I'm not alone out there, but I sometimes feel as if the entire universe is squarely upon my shoulders. Responsibility for shaping my life is greater than ever before, since my father's gone. I am next in line. An irretrievable piece of my being was lost with Dad's death. I am diminished. I will expand in my own good time, but, in any case, my life will never be quite the same without Harold Alexander Towle. I never thought I would be without my

Dad. He was invincible, wasn't he?

Well, before I become too maudlin, let me close, Chris, with a couple anecdotes to illustrate the bittersweet nature of my Dad's departure. Since his death came on Christmas Eve, my soul will never fail to remember that with the birth of Jesus arrived the slaughter of innocent children by Herod, an incident we conveniently smother in tinsel and evergreens. But the original Christmas story was not unadulterated merriment. It was instead a time of great poignance—profound joy and piercing loss. The timing of my father's death will constantly remind me to pay homage to the original Christmas which honored as holy both being born and dying.

The other anecdote relates to someone we both know, Chris. My father's dearest friend, George Nichol, who is also your brother Jeff's wife's grandfather, gave my Dad pajamas for that Christmas. Dad never got to wear them, but I did. Actually when I opened up the box with my mother on the Christmas morning following Dad's death, I found two pairs. I gave the first pair to our daughter, Erin, a teenager who adores large, baggy outfits, and I took the second pair to wear for myself. Although I was clearly swimming in them, for Dad had generated a much larger girth than I, I never felt more at home in pajamas than that Christmas night when I donned the special pair of pajamas which Dad neither saw nor wore. I put them on, looked in the mirror, cried my heart inside out, then crawled into bed, sleeping fitfully yet gratefully, snuggled inside my father's spacious, spanking-new PJ's!

And, so thank you, Chris, for consoling me with arms and words during this time of mourning. And for being my letter-writing and letter-reading buddy. There is no higher test of friendship than staying close and offering your love during times of grievous loss.

Your friend,
Tom

Men's group

Dear Tom,

I missed you at our last men's meeting at Dave's house. And yet I can't really say that the group was incomplete. We never lack for talkers, do we? And, we never lack for non-talkers, either. The upcoming Men's Renewal Weekend was discussed both generally ("I'm really looking forward to the men in our church getting closer . . . ") and specifically ("Should men be allowed to have sex during the weekend?"). How that last statement can exist in parentheses is truly a quirk of the written word! It was anything but parenthetical when it was spoken last Sunday evening.

Our men–minus–you group had a great meal and time together. During the evening discussion, there surfaced some misunderstandings and anger. Creatures of the deep—needing air, sunlight, or maybe just a break from the inner stink-dom. When anger has come up before in our group, I have felt the presence of some force that my mind immediately labeled "sinister" or "evil." Even, "the devil."

Strange how I've branded "anger" as anathema. And isn't it strange how archetypes of our religious heritage—"devil," for instance—seem to penetrate even the most guarded, liberal minds (now, that's an interesting word combination!) and nestle into our consciousness. I'm quite sure that my mental shelves are absolutely crowded with images and creatures that I have no reason to believe in. In fact, "no reason" (although too abstract to sport fangs, horns, extra legs, or a single, large, red eye) may be my biggest monster of all. "Wrestling with demons"—a wonderful phrase you use—comes to mind.

So, O.K. Having banished it to a distant mindscape long ago, I'm still wary of anger. I haven't placed a candle in the window but I sense a homecoming. And there may be several other lumbering forms coming up the path. I have never been comfortable with anger but, recently, I have sensed a change. I'm getting . . . better? Yes, I'm sure "better" is the right word.

Some guys are good with car engines, others never remember from week to week where the hood latch is. Some guys can write poetry, most can't. Some guys can, in a moment, get their blood pressure up, tighten their whole body, turn red, let loose with a hot breath, stinging with noise, and then, on the return breath, smooth the face and loosen the body, and a new balance prevails. A full storm cycle. A full blooming. By the way, I can't do that last trick. Parallel sentence construction dictated that divulgence.

Talk to you soon.

Love,
Chris

Charity of anger

Dear Chris,

Your recent letter centered upon anger—a theme dear to my heart yet elusive to my grasp. If I were to name the single emotion most difficult for me to give or receive, it would be anger. It sounds like we shoulder similar legacies in that respect.

In any case, I am often frustrated with others, occasionally indignant with them, but I seldom confess to my anger, rarely allowing others to feel the brunt of my raw wrath.

Naturally, I have read innumerable books arguing the charity of anger. I am aware of distinctions between anger and hostility, appropriate and inappropriate venting. But such knowledge has seldom made it easier for me to show rage myself. "Anger" has always loomed one short letter away from "danger" in my imagination.

I can locate two reasons to explain my *dis-ease* with anger: 1) There were no male models in my upbringing who directly displayed anger. I resemble my father's soft, passive demeanor. 2) I desire to stay in control of my emotions; anger might disrupt my equilibrium and throw everything out of whack.

I have come a long ways, Chris. I can now engage in arguments, as long as things remain reasonably respectful. Furthermore, I am better at confronting work associates and counselees instead of only soothing them. But I essentially remain a neophyte when anger surfaces or nasty feelings well up. Free-flowing bile still frightens me.

As you noted, I frequently use the phrase "wrestling with demons." It is a wonderful one, to be sure, but my wrestling tends to be more intellectual and verbal than emotional. I marvel at Jacob in the Hebrew scriptures actually spending an entire night in the throes of a wrestling match. I cheer him when he emerges triumphant yet limping. His bravery is a model for weak-spirited me. My interpersonal pacifism, while a sound and transformative philosophy, has also allowed me to tolerate wrongs, stay out of necessary battles, avoid the harsh edges of deepening intimacy.

I sometimes confuse gentleness with cowardice. I have lapsed into chicken-heartedness on more than one occasion in my persistent quest to be the "good guy." Adrienne Rich writes: "I am tired of faintheartedness." So am I, especially in myself, when the moral stakes are high.

Chris, as I reflect upon the image of wrestling I recall two men in D.H. Lawrence's novel, *Women in Love*, rough-housing. I don't remember the particulars, only that it was physical and fun. There was nothing overtly sexual, degrading or scary in this man-to-man encounter. It wasn't combat; it was a rare example of rousing, playful interaction between males.

Maybe I can learn to spar and wrangle, physically and emotionally, with women and men, in unhurtful, non-threatening ways as I grow up and on. I hope so.

Your friend,
Tom

"Nothing overtly sexual"

Dear Tom,

I had to respond to your allusion to the wrestling scene in *Women in Love*. Along with liking Bette Davis movies, being in charge of decorations for the high school prom, and always having girls as my best friends, my wide-eyed appreciation of this scene should have convinced me I was gay long before I finally did wake up to that inevitable realization.

Nothing overtly sexual, you say? I admit I had not read the novel before I saw the movie but as soon as I did I pawed my way through every page, desperate to find the written version of that mesmerizing, life-changing wrestling scene. Discussing the movie afterwards, I deferred to my friends (literature majors who *had* read the novel) even though my reactions were both numerous and powerful. During that time in my life as a closeted gay man, I pulled strong emotions and experiences down into the deepest corners of my being where they received some brutal, revisionist form of archiving. Maybe that's why now, so many recollections feel like they're brand new, happening again. And yet others almost seem beyond reclaiming, dull echoes instead of living memories.

I'm no literature scholar and I can't really recall what my friends said about the wrestling scene. I do remember they were more impressed with the fig-eating scene in which Alan Bates relishes the luscious, fleshy pulp of a ripe fig to the amusement and titillation of his table companions. D.H. Lawrence introduced wholly new sexual and emotional imagery into his writing. His style was fresh and relentless, hammering away at conventional values and perceptions. All of his images conveyed deeper truths—truths long hidden, long closeted. The fig. The wrestling match. So many others. I think he wrote in a way that challenged an entire culture to come out of the closet. Gee, I'm going to read that book again!

So back to your assessment: "nothing overtly sexual." Without getting into it, let me just say that I found the scene very sexual, very arousing, and, on a deeper level, revelatory. I believe D.H. Lawrence had every intention of infusing that scene with sexual power—the blazing fire, the food and wine, the locked door, the command not to be disturbed, the stripping of clothes. In the story, the two men had already expressed affection for one another and the narrative (always omniscient and often voyeuristic) detailed stronger forces pulling them together. Just before the incident, Birkin had botched a marriage proposal to Ursula and then sought the comfort of Gerald's companionship. And I could go on. I don't doubt that you saw nothing sexual in the scene, Tom, but . . . the scene was very sexual from where I sat. No genital penetration, I agree, but rereading the passage I doubt that flesh could press much closer.

Let me anticipate a couple reactions you, or someone else more likely, might have. First, gay men are often accused of think-ing every situation has gay overtones. Admittedly we do bring our own values with us when we read a book or appreciate a film. As a closeted gay man, I allowed myself to perceive through art what my eyes continually averted in real life. Art as truth serum. Art as reality therapy.

Second, gay men have also been accused of thinking every good-looking straight man is just a seduction away from "turning gay." Well, I don't believe that and, besides, any scientific study would be fraught with too many problems. I may on occasion see the world through lavender-colored glasses but far more often I have had blinders on (or had them put on) while people, places, and great works of literature that *do* relate to the gay experience are misinterpreted or misunderstood.

I said I *had* to respond. More response than I thought, actu-ally. Gay pride has spoken, huh? In conclusion, Tom, I find your appraisal, "not overtly sexual," believable from your point of view. But from my perspective, highly unlikely. D.H. and I just wanted you to know how we felt about this one.

Love,
Chris

Homosensual

No, I am not going to bed with him, I have been brainwashed by the "sexualists." My true problem, rather, is what to do with my *tenderness* toward him. How to remain honest in the expression of my love without having any desire to resort to sexual behavior or even imagery. For, indeed, what I feel toward him and want to express cannot be expressed sexually.

Perhaps the Hindus are right. They have a more complex theory of human energies and the body. Where we up-to-date moderns emphasize only sex and aggression, they understand many types of energy playing on our bodies. Sex and aggression, yes, but also tenderness, sheer vitality, purely mental energy, creative energy, contemplative energy.

Stuart Miller

Dear Chris,

The Greeks claimed that the essence of genuine friendship was intellectual discourse or weighty conversation. As one who traffics daily with the healing power of words, I don't undervalue enlightening dialog for a minute. But it is my experience that friendships among men are eased into the deeper places and sustained over the long haul by physicality—touching one another with safe, firm, tender hands.

The biggest taboo in male culture is physical touch, intimacy. We men have wrestled and boxed with one another, playfully and viciously, throughout history. We have beaten, even killed, one another in hand-to-hand combat. But sharing positive, warm sentiments via bodily contact remains an exceptional exchange for most men. As Sam Keen notes: "The unspoken rule of our culture is that it is all right for one man to touch another to give pain but not pleasure."

We are changing, to be sure. Men are hugging more naturally and frequently. We heterosexuals can occasionally kiss another man—the right man, like our father, son, or friend—without excessive blushing. In short, we are learning in fits and spurts how to be close and erotic without being sexual.

A brief yet breakthrough experience for me, Chris, occurred way back in 1971 at a minister's conference in Palm Desert, California when we went dancing at a local restaurant nightclub one evening. There were mainly ministers and mates at our annual event, but some of us were present without our partners.

There were more men than women in our group. The music was upbeat, danceable. My feet were itching to get out on the floor and cut a caper, but all the women were taken. I didn't want to butt in on one of our couples, so I spontaneously asked Gene to join me in a fast, free-form swirl. He agreed.

We gamboled around the floor for a half hour or so. The experience was certainly new for both of us, practicing heterosexuals, somewhat awkward, but not embarrassing. Neither Gene nor I felt any sexual tug toward each other. We were simply having a jolly, good time.

The manager of the club had seen enough, felt enough, imagined enough. He came over and asked us to leave. We resisted awhile, countering with comments like: "Women dance together here at the club. What's the difference?" Or "come on now, we just blend in on this compact dance floor with women and men moving about in their own worlds anyway." The manager blurted back: "I don't care. I want you faggots out. You're gross and unnatural! Leave, now, or I'll call the police."

Gene, being a relentless social protester, got irked and carried the debate to the limits, but to no avail. The battle lost, our innocent fun left for memory, Gene and I, then our whole group, disappeared into the night.

Whenever we men relate to one another with unconventional physicality, however playful and innocent, people's (usually other men's) homophobia goes wild. They are repelled by two men exhibiting harmless, frolicking affection. They envision genital sexuality. This judgmental response should come as no surprise, for our human fears and attractions feed one another, residing closer to the surface than we ever admit.

Chris, in men's retreats I will often, after hours of emotional discourse and profound sharing, invite men to pair up, and ask them, alternately, to massage one another's hands. After fifteen minutes of giving and receiving such fundamental physical sustenance, the partners wind down by serenely, softly holding each other's hands for a couple minutes. Then, if and when they choose, I invite them to talk about what it meant for each to share in this "touching" exercise.

What do we men find? We discover that our homophobic fears are lessened by hand massaging, a relatively comfortable way to be physically close with the same-sex. We learn that when we caringly knead the skin and flesh of another man, we grow less likely to consider injuring men, women, children, or earth ever again. We move inexorably toward becoming the stewards and husbandmen we were created to be.

For me, Chris, the most helpful distinctions I make and practice are those which my colleague Ron Mazur makes between being *social* (formal encounters), being *sensual* (physical affection), and being *sexual* (genital behavior). The first two areas I enjoy with men; the third one I don't.

I choose to be social with men whom I meet for the first time or relate to in a business fashion or in whom I have modest continuing interest. I relate sensually toward a growing number of male friends, family members, and associates. I do not engage in same-sex genital behavior, so the third zone, genital intimacy, is offbounds for me.

Each of us, as adult men, is accountable for selecting, then enfleshing, our relational behaviors. My goal is to be homosensual with respect to men whom I enjoy, expanding my repertoire of sensory responses appropriate to each bond.

My operative rule remains simple and clear: when either of us squirms, I stop the gesture.

Your friend,
Tom

Small gift

Dear Tom,

I just got your wonderful letter. I know that I will read it many times. I have so many reactions.

Your letters always brim with riches and, yet, in the middle of such wealth I realize how long it's been since I wrote to you. I have felt a similar frustration all my life: arrogant certainty on the one hand—that I can tackle anything and do it well; and, on the other, tremendous despair and doubt—what do I have to do this time, where will the energy come from, why can't I just sleep? But there is a third component as well, and this is the new excitement in my life. That new thing is "I can talk to Tom about this." I can face up to both my feeling of confidence and its (evil) twin, despair. Who would have thought these pageant-play cast members could sit at the table (the "head" table?) together and their separateness dissolve? This spirit of resolution now graces my life—occasionally. And I am thankful.

Tom, I may not be the best correspondent in the world but remembering my solitary days leads me to believe I'm a strong candidate for "most improved." The body of written work you have created over the past two years is, in a word, intimidating. The anxiety of all this, however, pales in comparison to the despair that I would feel if I didn't talk to you about it. Again, that's the difference in my life. I know that I *need* to talk about these things and I'm beginning to know that I *can* talk about them.

I've said enough for now. I want to put something into your gentle hands that comes from my own. It's a small gift.

There are so many flowers in the garden. The sun shines as brightly on the peony as on the rose. Each gift of color and fragrance fills the open heart. I strive to live with an open heart, Tom, and your gifts strengthen me. Thank you.

Love,
Chris

More heart-talk

Be slow to fall into friendship, but when thou art in,
continue firm and constant.

Socrates

Dear Chris,

I want to respond to three phrases in your last epistle.

"I can talk to Tom about this . . . "

Being talk-mates is at the heart of our being revolutionary
friends. There is no greater tribute to our kinship than to know
that when one of us is stuck, hurt, or elated, we will convey the
need or news to our brother.

I stand ready and eager to give and receive the widely ranging stirrings of our hearts.

" . . . in a word, intimidating."

So, my writing output in recent years intimidates you. Okay,
I hear you. Well, my friend, singing next to you has intimidated
me royally over the years, yet our musical collaborations have oc-
casioned pleasurable moments of the highest order for me.

Therefore, I urge us to risk wobbling but resist falling in our
writing collegiality. Chris, our co-creation, this volume of essays
and letters, has already proven a treasure trove precisely because
of our variant styles and distinct views. I particularly cherish,
without attempting to imitate, the flow of your allusive language
and naturalistic details. I major in concepts rather than images, so
ours is an enriching, expansive mix.

If we are brave enough to plumb our spirits and venture
our true sentiments, I worry not about the resulting creation. We
won't intimidate one another or anybody else peering in from the
outside if we remain true to ourselves and caring of one another.
As Auchincloss remarked about the friendship of Byron and
Shelley:

The two men were too different as poets ever to influence each other in any matter of style, treatment or even subject matter. They did something more important: they inspired each other. Each found excitement and stimulation in the other's genius. They warmed their writing hands, so to speak, at each other's fire.

When all is said, done, and written, may our friendship be warmed at each other's fire too.

"It's a small gift."

I beg to differ, buddy. Our gifts may be clumsily conveyed, and short in length, but never small. I have never yet failed to be enlarged by the gifts of your heart and horizon.

Finally, Chris, I feel a pep talk coming on and ask your indulgence. Our friendship, any friendship, will never enjoy the socially sanctioned benefits and hoopla of public ceremony. We aren't likely to bless our bond with a refined celebration. Our friendship won't make the society page of the newspaper and won't be recorded with the County Clerk. Yet our friendship, despite society's seeming indifference, is terribly real and profoundly nourishing.

Our friendship has consisted of calls, regularly scheduled engagements, shared projects, serendipitous contacts, special events where one of us is center stage and the other cheers on the sidelines, and perhaps, most of all, our faithful (for the most part) correspondence. Chris, our friendship shows abundant evidence of careful cultivation, a regular supply of affection and truth telling.

Sufficient nutriment.

Your friend,
Tom

Touchstone

Dear Tom,

There's comfort in just holding a pen. It's a comfort that you've felt as well. As pen hovers above fresh paper, I'm often overwhelmed with the possibilities—the unlimited potential for creation. Do creations wait in line somewhere? Do they anticipate their own release, their own birth? Do they sit anxiously, hoping I or some other soul will stumble upon a code of scratches that defines one of them? No, I think not. *Midsummer Night's Dream* is too fresh to have languished in some Valley of Oblivion before Shakespeare "called its number." And *Dandelion Wine* (a personal favorite) is too unique to have developed anywhere but in Ray Bradbury's fertile mind.

And so it is with your writing, Tom. Your letters, sermons, and conversations have no doubt benefited from a wash of images and an endless spate of words that you've absorbed your whole life. But the sentences and thoughts are your own. Like all acts of creation, your writing helps keep the universe forever new.

The line of communication between you and me is itself a unique path. In exploring my truths I need to have a singular audience—a friend to listen. Together, two friends create a spiritual touchstone that measures their words. You and I share many thoughts and ideas. But that's not to say they all have the same weight or value. Personal communication is a real smorgasbord —pettiness alongside the magnanimous, whining side by side with the profound.

Sometimes our touchstone can help us sort out the barrage of words. Sort them into two piles: rings and thuds. What do I mean by rings and thuds? Well, some of our communication comes from the heart, untainted by a mood or a grudge or a lapse of judgment. Those would be "rings"—as in a clear-sounding bell. The other communications, with less noble origins, would be "thuds." As in, you tried to hit the bell and get a clear-sounding ring but you smashed something next to it and the true value of the communication is given the announcement it deserves—a dull thud.

"Ring!"—a truth is uttered, a deeply held secret unfurls its wings, a long hidden pain reveals itself. "Thud!"—I let loose with a spiteful remark, an 8x10 glossy passes as a candid snapshot, an anecdote once again has me climbing the victory stand or, perhaps just as common, has me relegated to the attic, awaiting the fire that will consume me *and* my tragic madness.

We share plenty of both, I imagine. I'm wondering if we can tune our ears to hear the accompanying "ring" or "thud" for each thought. And then I wonder if we really should try to get rid of all the thuds. That would be censorship of the worst kind! Friends need to air their minds and hearts. In a friendship, "thuds" should be as welcome as "rings."

My letters will inevitably be sprinkled with "rings" and "thuds." I announce for all the world to hear that I have flaws. A flawed self can generate through spoken and written communication a true reflection, but that reflection would have to include the flaws. Thuds along with the rings.

Conversely, the rings and thuds (by example and counterexample) suggest some model of perfection. But perfection is a cruel god and I choose not to enter its orbit. So I offer an alternative: authenticity. I know that you welcome authenticity as a more worthy goal than perfection. Authenticity is the language of the touchstone. Our touchstone affirms our individual and collective searches for authenticity. I want to hear both thuds and rings from our touchstone, Tom. And if I grow weary of my own search, I can still be a witness to yours.

Keep writing—rings and thuds—and I will too. I've got a lot of both to do.

Love,
Chris

Like all acts of creation

Dear Chris,

"Like all acts of creation, writing helps keep the universe forever new."
In writing, we become co-creators. From original dreams, we spawn fresh thoughts. Our insides dance in the open air.

In writing, men come our closest to giving birth.

In writing, we give back praise, upset, and hope to the cosmos which so graciously loved us into existence and continues to grant us daily bread and breath.

"Thuds along with the rings."
I asked myself the other day whether or not I would choose to live a life void of clanking sounds, losses, thuds. I realized that even if given the opportunity for unadulterated bliss, I would turn it down. That's why the notion of "heaven" as an eternal resting place has never thrilled me.

If we cut off despair, we cut off hope. Joy loses its edge without the possibility of its partner, sorrow. If there were no clouds, we wouldn't enjoy the sun. I agree with 19th Century religious forebear Theodore Parker: "As I look back over my life, I find no disappointment and no sorrow I could afford to lose . . . "

According to an ancient legend, a woman came to the river Styx, to be ferried to the land of departed spirits. Charon, the ferryman, reminded her of her privilege to drink of the waters of Lethe, which grant forgetfulness of the life she was leaving.

"I will forget how I have suffered," she exclaimed.

"Yes," replied Charon, "and also how you have rejoiced."

"I will forget how I have been hated."

"And also," said Charon, "how you have been loved."

After much thought, the woman left the waters of Lethe untasted.

Better the mingled memories of suffering and sorrow, joy and love, clarity and muddleness, thuds and rings, than oblivion.

Your friend,
Tom

Waiting and Prancing

In this next set of letters, Chris and I visit various regions of our respective souls—both light and heavy, reflective and revealing, about sports and cowboys, pieces awash with light and others immersed in the shadow of death.

Here you will find the two of us speaking from experiences that happen away from our friendship. Our separateness makes being together more special.

Sharing our different experiences through letters and conversation keeps our friendship awake. Our friendship percolates and deepens.

Here we are—waiting and prancing.

My waiting room

Dear Tom,

Sitting and waiting. There's an image. Not just an image but a reality for too many of us.

I talk about "living my dream" when I stage my singing concerts. Now, in my thirties, I feel like I'm finally embracing something uniquely important to me. My life has included lots of "things that are important to me"—career, school, friends, politics, religion—but they are not *uniquely* important to me. Singing brings my life together. It challenges me to conspire with my best energies and my deepest, singular reality. Other "important" things contribute but, without some deep unifying force, my life would remain fragmented.

Chris—worker, scholar, friend, activist, church member. How about: Chris—singer.

So how does sitting and waiting pertain to living my dream? Well, consider a waiting room—sort of an archetypal waiting room. In my mind, this room is easy to conjure up. Perhaps because it's so ordinary. You know how anthropologists tell us that certain icons and symbols appear in diverse cultures? Well, my waiting room may seem tied to Western culture, but I'm convinced that, if it's not already in our species' lexicon of myth and symbol, it's on a short list of candidates eligible for the next round of voting. Yes, that's right, this is actually a promotional letter to add "waiting room" to humankind's (higher?) consciousness.

The waiting room. Let me take you on a tour. One door leads into the room; another door is on the far wall. Presumably, the second door leads beyond, to our goals. Chairs are all around, set against off-white walls hung with innocuous florals. A counter suggests the possibility of activity behind its gray Formica surface but evidence of such activity is absent. No one else is in the room. My behavior is automatic, automatonish. Perhaps I am cued by the physical surroundings, relaxed by the almost inaudible music, and taken in by the apparent security, comfort, and ordinariness of it all.

The absence of others never raises a question in my mind. After all, why should anyone else be there? This waiting room is my waiting room—universal icon to the contrary. My acts are relatively passive—walking in, sitting down. I rise to study the pictures, to peek nonchalantly over the counter, to walk close to the second door, straining to detect some noise.

Then someone pokes their head in, their feet planted outside and hands braced against the doorknob and frame. "Did you know this is a waiting room?" he asks. I nod silently—eyes round, mouth loose. "That no one's in charge of?" the almost-visitor continues. The muscles around my eyes tighten and my stomach begins a slow roll. "That leads nowhere? That's a waste of time?" His incredulity rises with his eyebrows. My outer response betrays bafflement—a gaping mouth and even tinier eyes. Inside, my soul nods wisely, signaling a lesson finally learned by this earthly shell.

With a terse, "OK. As long as you know," my visitor disappears. My heart aches and I momentarily crave the unconsciousness of these many chairs that share my way station.

Once we *know* about our waiting rooms—their seduction, illusion, and disruption of life—the next move is our own. We can't wait for someone to lead us out of our own waiting room. My next move was obvious. I walked out the door I came in. I doubt if the second door even had hinges. Who cares? I knew the first door would get me out. The trip beyond the waiting room sometimes requires retracing a few steps.

Do you have a waiting room, Tom?

Love,
Chris

P.S. Please sign and circulate the enclosed petition to add "waiting room" to Humankind's Psychic Lexicon.

Prancing in the stall

Dear Chris,

Your writing is poetic, richly figurative and markedly distinct from my prosy style. You paint word-pictures; I emote, talk, think out loud. How lovely to juxtapose our dissimilar offerings.

I don't have much of a "waiting room," Chris. I seldom wait for anything if I can help it. I would be better off if I pondered more, sat still, waited my heart's turn, rather than eternally racing around.

My proclivity is to keep churning, stay in motion. My self-delusion is that if I am busy, I must be productive. I tend to confuse sheer activity with results.

The story goes that once a horse has been trained to race, it is always ready to run when the bugle sounds. If a horse is injured or for some reason cannot run, it will nevertheless prance in the stall when it hears the bugle.

You describe yourself as "relatively passive" in your waiting room. I prance about restlessly in my stall whether or not I am on tap to race.

You from your waiting room and I from my stall . . . are exchanging notes, bridging our disparate worlds.

Your friend,
Tom

I will whisper

Dear Tom,

On the afternoon of Bob Jepperson's memorial service, my thoughts are like . . .

the sand

choppy from too many footsteps, casting tiny
shadows across tiny valleys

how the sand must yearn for a high tide to smooth
its troubled face

the seaweed

a chunk of some great kelp bed has broken off and
washed to shore

where it is now chewed relentlessly between wave
and sand

these men

sharing the beach with me on this fall afternoon

single, silent, staring, starving

stirring and then still, stalking and then sulking

Losing someone always hits us where we are raw. Is it any wonder that we try to protect ourselves? Is it any surprise that we bandage ourselves against the pain? That we hope the rawness will go away and be replaced with tougher skin? There are some places where we are always raw. How we fear and feel betrayed by this point of vulnerability!

Why can't we learn that it too is an important part of our being? We never fully live until we accept it—this invisible organ that resonates with every birth and with every death. If we began to really listen, could we live with its pulse, its pounding rhythm? Would it drive us mad? Or does it drive us mad when we ignore it?

When our own life dissolves into this rawness, our only hope is to befriend it—to love and accept ourselves completely.

I've been singing a song to myself over and over this afternoon. Tonight, I will offer it as a part of Bob's memorial service, "I Will Whisper Your Name." The song did well on the country charts this past summer and, although it's a simple, pop song—written for a wedding, I think—I find wonderfully touching and warm sentiments in its simple structure. I've whispered Bob's name several times today.

Through our voices—whether singing, whispering, talking, or even writing words on paper—love becomes manifest. "May love be the spirit of this church . . . " I'll see you and Carolyn and the rest of Bob's family of friends tonight.

Love,
Chris

The shadow of death

As Hamlet lies dying, he begs Horatio to carry on: "If thou didst ever hold me in thy heart, absent thee from felicity awhile and draw thy breath in pain to tell my story."

William Shakespeare

The friend I can trust is the one who will let me have my death. The rest are actors who want me to stay and further the plot.

Adrienne Rich

Dear Chris,

We've lost and continue to lose mutual friends to the implacable foe of AIDS. I am undone every time you sing your soul-wrenching rendition of "We Shall Overcome" sandwiched around "Abraham, Martin and John," a ballad which recalls the devastating assassinations of Abraham Lincoln, Martin Luther King, Jr., John F. Kennedy as well as Robert Kennedy. Near the end of the song you reel off the first names of friends, brothers, sons, and lovers—persons known in our San Diego community—who have perished because of the dread disease. The names are usually of men, but not always.

In Jewish teaching there are three ascending levels of how one mourns: with tears, that's the lowest; with silence, that is higher; and with a song, that is the highest. Perhaps during these confusing, angry, helpless times of a plague, we mourn most fully when we sing our hearts inside out. It is our best defense and our fullest release.

I am thinking of death today, because I just lost a church member and personal friend to a brain tumor. He was my age and a few years older than you. His death marked the shocking and rapid decline to a vigorous, buoyant person.

I pray that you will not get AIDS, Chris. I don't want you to die now. You are flourishing in beautiful ways. Our friendship has many moons to view before it must end in sadness, with the death of one of us.

The most important thing we do in life is to love and be loved. We love, because we know we will lose one another someday.

Someday, yes, but not soon, not soon.

Your friend,
Tom

Airports and cowboys

Dear Tom,

There's something both disturbing and safe about an airport. I've had the feeling many times before—one of those familiar feelings that predates my visiting airports, I suppose. My friend Steve and I just concluded a wonderful week in Santa Fe. We just said good-bye—rather simply. Both too weary to express all that the week has meant to us. Steve now heads for San Francisco and I wait these last thirty minutes with few things to distract me from this "airport" feeling. Maybe it's a suspension of feeling. It's a feeling complete with soundtrack: footsteps on a brick floor, a television set in the lounge pushing football, occasional bursts of cheerful greeting when a flight arrives as the rest of us, slightly annoyed, wait for the clamor to be absorbed into the muffled hubbub of this way station. This place drives me into a state of passive battiness! Where is the plane?

I'm on the plane. I've tried to work up some romantic interest in each of the three stewards as they reveal themselves one by one in the course of their over-rehearsed duties. It's not working. I feel nothing for these men. How I hunger for infatuation! How I miss it! I suffer an impotence that expresses itself in the disparity between what I crave and what I feel. Let's up the ante from infatuation to love. How I miss loving someone! For a quick moment, I shudder at what the lack of loving in my life might suggest—a spiritual impotence of much grander proportions. I calm my racing breath with a chant. You can love! You can love! You can love! On this day in late October, my pre-flight mantra returns me to the suspended, cocoon-like feeling.

My week. I want to tell you about it. I may tie all this together yet. Last Saturday, Steve and I rendezvoused in Albuquerque, rented a car, and drove up to Santa Fe. We stopped at his friend Brian's for a quick check-in. Looking back, I know that Brian was a big part of my week. He's a writer, a singer, a man of great wit and gentleness . . . and a person with advanced ARC, AIDS-related complex. Steve and Brian have been friends for over ten years. I gather (from the nuts and berries of casual conversation) that Brian once had a crush on Steve. Eighteen months ago, during a weekend swim meet, I did, too.

Brian's fall into grace happened in a San Francisco discotheque; mine, on a pool deck. Both of our crushes, triggered by Steve's handsome visage and cool demeanor, have now evolved and we each find ourselves blessed with Steve's friendship, rather than a romantic involvement.

A friendship between Brian and me has now begun. Soulmate is often thrown around but here the label really fits. We talked a lot, sharing stories of childhood, adulthood, gay experiences, singing, writing, aspirations, anxieties. Nothing seemed off limits. His sense of humor and deeply ingrained gentleness and goodness wrapped our verbal explorations with a comfort I rarely feel. I want to tell you more about Brian on our next run. You'd like him, too.

For now, how about a letter within a letter? My thoughts of friendship and romance cause me to pull out a special postcard from a stack that never got sent this past week.

> To the Cowboy on a Postcard,
>
> Your picture has captured my heart. I explore every corner and both sides of the card for more information about you. No name, much less an address and phone number. I don't know who you are or where you came from. And yet, I've always known you were there. "Out There."
>
> You gaze through the camera and into my eyes. It's like cruising for the disconnected, the dispossessed. At times like this, I understand the attractiveness of pornography. You are not even present, you don't know me, yet the interaction—between man and postcard—seems strangely complete. If you did dream of someone in your "out there," I doubt that I would fit the image you held in your heart. But I can't afford to include your dreams and your needs in my fantasy. I play both sides. Yes, strangely complete.

What a picture I would be to you! A Sony Walkman pumps cabaret music into my head and I'm sipping red wine. You and I "met" in Santa Fe. I was thumbing through a stack of calendars—lots of portly Indian matrons in one, anthropomorphic coyotes in another. None of them were reduced in price or even that intriguing. And then there was you . . .

I walked over to the postcard rack and there you were—a stack so full in the card holder that I congratulated myself on being the very first to find you. Somehow that was important. You were (and still are) wearing a hat. A heavy, long-sleeved shirt hangs over broad, relaxed shoulders and a tobacco tin etches a crease in the pocket over your heart. A large belt buckle pulls a strap tight around a trim waist. Strong, round thumbs hook over a leather thong holding a pair of chaps over your denim-clad legs. Folds in the pant legs and stiffer folds of boot leather carry the dust from a full day of cow-punching, fence-mending, cactus-spine-pulling, and brow-wiping.

About here, I pick up where the card leaves off.

It's the end of the day. You're home. As you remove your hat, I admire its shape, its incongruous whiteness, and its closeness to you. You take it off with great tenderness. We look at it in your hands for a brief moment and then at each other, silently agreeing the hat is a sacred friend. You hang it alongside the ropes and tackle on the wall. Off with the chaps, each leather strap sliding seductively across your sunburned hands. I cajole you into an easy chair, pull off your boots, undo the silver belt buckle (your one concession to ornament), and slip off the pants, shirt, and everything else that stands between us—save the dust, sweat, and two-days' growth of beard. Not mine. I shaved a half hour ago when I heard Napoleon barking at the end of the road and looked out to see you gliding above a cloud of dust.

Don't ask about my day. Not a word about yours. Begin our day now. Holding and being held, breathing and listening, searching and finding, wanting and getting, needing the other more than the self. It all blurs into bliss.

On the next morn, we can't let each other go. Finally, the light grows, the bladders plead for release, one of us farts, and the day begins. Getting dressed, putting on the chaps and the hat, I then wait at the door for a lusty hug before going out on the trail. I'm happy to do it. If for nothing else, just for the pleasure of seeing your manliness in the dawn—barefoot, with flattened hair and a kimono hastily pulled about your square shoulders.

Our friendship, Tom, grows alongside other friendships and romances—real or imagined—in my life. Our friendship is between a gay man and a straight man. Different from a friendship between straight men, perhaps. But as we talk about our lives, we discover again and again our common humanity—beyond gay and straight. Our expression of that overarching, underlying humanity can also take different forms. I want to share things about being gay with you, Tom, to the extent that you desire it and that it's comfortable. I know I haven't pushed the limits in this letter; "pushing the limits" is not really my interest. But that's not to say our sharing will always be comfortable. As long as we stand together in our willingness to reveal our lives to each other, the differences will only enhance our friendship, not diminish it.

See you soon, it'll be good to get home and run with you this week.

Love,
Chris

Let's up the ante

Dear Chris,

"Let's up the ante from infatuation to love."

What an incisive piece of self-analysis! In fact, your terse invitation sums up the purpose of life. We humans spend our entire lives navigating the waters from foolish, immature clinging to measured, passionate commitments . . . from infatuation to love.

We die somewhere along the passage.

"To the cowboy on a postcard . . . "

Your fantasy captured my interest, but not my heart. I welcomed your touching, sensual excitement.

Being married, utterly attached and incurably devoted, I reside in a different zone than you, a single man currently available for new encounters and developing partnerships. I confess that even cowgirls seldom give this mid-lifer much of a thrill anymore, because romancing my wife more than occupies my body and soul.

The postcard fantasies I collect are of the sensuous hills of Italy and the lush colors of New Zealand's landscape.

This difference keeps our friendship invigorating.

"Pushing the limits is not really my interest."

It's not mine either, friend. We both, by temperament and conviction, happen to be nice rather than nasty guys. For better or worse, we just aren't abrasive types. I sometimes wonder if there is sufficient sandpaper in our relationship. Oh, we shove one another once and awhile, mystify and bother one another upon occasion, but that's about the extent of our disharmony.

Should our friendship contain more agitation or harshness? Does our native sweetness run the risk of producing a syrupy, cloying bond over the long haul? Blake claimed that "Opposition is true friendship." Well, can we be opposites without sliding into full-bore opposition? I think so, I hope so.

Right now, Chris, our friendship isn't any less rich because we are kindly sorts. Yet we must always strive to be warm without turning saccharine, firm rather than flimsy, brave enough to risk difficult truths in trust.

Your friend,
Tom

Doubly blessed

> We have only begun to know the power that is in us
> if we would join our solitudes in the communion of
> struggle. So much is unfolding that must complete its
> gesture. So much is in bud.
>
> Denise Levertov

Dear Chris,

Even though we aren't professionals who work together daily, I consider you my colleague. We run together. We sing together. We write together. We share hurts and hopes. Ours is what I call a "collaboration of psyches," even when we aren't laboring on a common project or residing in the same village.

We are yoked together in quest of a lovelier and holier life for ourselves and those around us. Ken Keyes has said that there are two kinds of encouragers in our existence: lovers and teachers. The lovers are necessary because they support us; the teachers, because they stretch our horizons.

Chris, I believe we are friends who love one another without being sexual partners and who transmit wisdom to each other without being licensed teachers. We are doubly blessed.

Our friendship is grounded in loving and teaching, generosity and appreciation. We nurture one another in a way that never seems like tit for tat, only natural reciprocity. I'm not interested in proving our friendship, just in being friends. Sometimes you push me, and other times I pull you. We are both initiators in our friendship, which brings to mind Samuel Johnson's cogent reflection: "Friendship is seldom lasting but between equals."

What escapades lie ahead for our friendship? Who knows? A protest march, a duet, another writing project, a brother–spirit conference? I care not, for so much is in bud. We will be buddies to the end, in ways beyond our predicting, even imagining.

Your friend,
Tom

The traveling church

Dear Tom,

Thanks for telling me you consider me a colleague. Yes, I do enjoy the company and sensibilities of ministers. And there has been ample speculation—both spoken and unspoken—about my suitability for the ministry. Although I'm honored I don't think I'll take that path. But, then I quickly consider the paths that I have chosen—singing and writing songs about life, love, and human rights; staging benefit concerts for a variety of causes; and actively participating in clubs, groups, and church communities besides my own. In this chosen work, largely without compensation, I *do* minister. Not as a professional but almost always with a full heart.

Speaking of colleagues, I accompanied our friend Terry last week who was asked to be a visiting minister at a small church in the desert. What a delightful woman! We had a lively discussion as we drove the part-desert, part-mountain terrain on our journey. We were a spiritual tag team that day—she would deliver a sermon; I would sing a couple of songs.

After we arrived at the church, I sat and watched a few of the early congregants moving about. They all had certain tasks to prepare for the service. Some embodied a buoyant spirit. Others held tight to gloomier moods. For some reason, I focused on the latter. Their chores became a backdrop for undirected pronouncements of theology, politics, and philosophy. What seemed like attempts at conversation fell short. Breathless, preoccupied, and aloof, the would-be communicators launched into chatter that seemed to define walls instead of paths. "Where is the love?" I thought. "Where is the intention to really connect?" I felt my own sense of well-being and connectedness slipping away.

I looked around for Terry and then remembered something she shared in the car earlier that morning. Before a sermon, she liked to go off somewhere to get centered. She asked what I did before singing. I claimed, "Not much," perhaps a bit too flippantly. Then I added that recently, prior to concert performances, I had taken to prayer.

"Prayer." The word was dropped gently. How would this bright, young, lesbian, embarking on a profession in the liberal ministry, respond. She lifted the word as gently as it had been placed between us. Great Spirit. God. Goddess. That which cannot be defined or encompassed. Comfort that came with surrendering control to a power beyond. These are the things we spoke of. These were the sounds of our hearts. And as I remembered our conversation a feeling of peace quietly enveloped me and I felt eager to hear Terry's sermon and to share my song.

My Sunday service had happened in a Volkswagen bug on a stretch of country road earlier that morning. Now, I focused on the song I would contribute as a part of Terry's service for these busy, sometimes connecting, sometimes colliding souls.

Love,
Chris

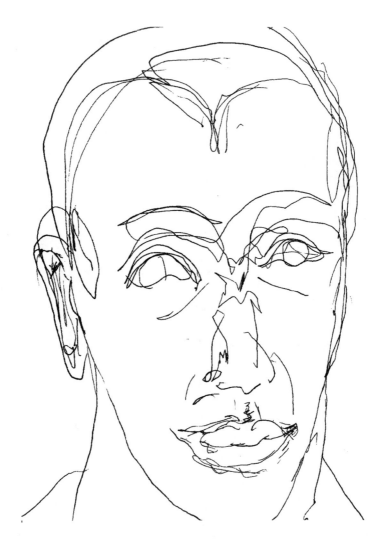

City of Friends

I dreamed in a dream I saw a city invincible to the attacks of the whole of the rest of the earth. I dreamed that was the new city of Friends. Nothing was greater there than the quality of robust love . . .

Walt Whitman

Chris and I love this quote by Walt Whitman. We feel that, in our friendship between a gay man and a straight man, we are helping to build "the new city of Friends." There is nothing exceptional about us personally, but we are engaged in an exceptional venture: brothers growing closer in affection and unity. The character Martin Dysart says in the play *Equus:*

In an ultimate sense I cannot know what I do in this place, yet I do ultimate things. Essentially I cannot know what I do, yet I do essential things.

Building durable, devoted friendships is one of the ultimate and essential things we humans do while occupying this earth.

"Robust" is a classically masculine term which refers to strong, large musculature and a rough, boisterous demeanor. Friendship demands a robustness of mind, faith and flavor, a hardiness of spirit and stoutness of heart. Ours is such a robust bond. Ours is a friendship where, as e.e. cummings noted, "2 + 2 is 5" because we generate a presence and possibilities larger than the two of us added together.

We saunter along the path of friendship. While we haven't reached our final destination, we have arrived at many a base camp, from which we have continued our mutually satisfying trek. Undoubtedly, we could be braver in sharing our upsets, without injuring one another; in sharing our wounds, without comparing them; in sharing our deeper dreams, without binding either of us to specific results. As one of our mutual buddies says, there are only opportunities in the world of befriending, no guarantees.

But this much I already know: we will never leave one another when our opinions might clash; we will console one another when we are down or sick; we will protect, stretch and be present for one another in fair or foul weather.

Meanwhile, we plug steadily along, writing one another letters, revealing our minds, and nurturing with words that travel from one heart to the other.

We're just friends!

> When a man becomes dear to me, I have touched
> the goal of fortune. I find very little written directly to
> the heart of this matter.
>
> Ralph Waldo Emerson

Dear Chris,

You know how people who are buddies will often say, "Well, we're *just* friends," implying that friendship is a partial, inferior, or transitional state. I feel strongly that friendship is valuable in and of itself, neither lesser nor greater than any other relational condition. It doesn't have to evolve into "love" or "romance" to be worthy or complete. It doesn't have to lead to anything other than itself. It is fine and fulfilling on its own merit.

Also, the word *just* doesn't simply mean *only*. It also means rightful, equitable, fitting, and suitable—words laden with power. *Just* is related to "justice" and, as such, reminds us that friendship is never purely a personal activity but always a political one as well. Friendships represent more than people yoked together. Genuine friendships are nourished by the intricate network of human relationships, and they contribute abundantly to the larger community.

Through growing our ties, you and I, Chris, participate in substantive, social change. We bring men closer together. We diminish the widespread, unchecked alienation between straights and gays. We contribute our fair share to make a fearful, unjust world somewhat more merciful and friendly, if you will. We are participating in the Copernican revolution in relationships which has the capacity to heal our broken world. Right (*just*) relations, as Buddhism recognizes, are exceedingly rare in the human sphere. Consequently, every living embodiment of "*just* friends" sustains coming generations and ennobles our universe.

Having invoked the words of Emerson and Buddha and as long as I'm off on a reflective jag, I would offer the wisdom of yet another great promoter of friendship, Aristotle, who delineated three benchmarks for a vital friendship.

First, Aristotle claims that there must be joy. Friends simply enjoy one another's company. We have done our share of celebrating through the years. I'm not sure we've ever engaged in mindless whoopee, but silliness, yes. When you "roasted" me, Chris, at my 50th birthday party, you were at your zaniest. I laughed tears.

Second, Aristotle notes that friends are those we help and who help us. Unilateral caregiving doesn't qualify as friendship. When you need me, Chris, you know I will show up. If I need your presence, I can count on you. And through it all, neither of us keeps score.

Third, our Greek forebrother felt that true friends "share a moral vision." Our friendship has served far more than our own ego satisfaction. We have touched the lives of our partners, our parents, gay and straight friends, and men and women in our community.

It is comforting to know that the greatest of our human tribe throughout history considered friendship among the highest of human pursuits and were themselves serious practitioners. We modern males perch upon their friendly shoulders.

Your friend,
Tom

The snake tattoo

Dear Tom,

I visited my friend Mike at the hospital. I asked if he had music to listen to. We both agreed there was nothing on that damned TV worth watching. It felt good to share that moment of disgust with him. Maybe it helped relieve some of the anger.

"What's that on your cheek?" I asked, reasonably sure the small, crusty eruptions weren't Kaposi's sarcoma. There were also some on his upper lip although they were being rapidly obscured by a new mustache. Michael grows a magnificent mustache. I've always admired it. That and his large, pale blue eyes. And the tattoo of a snake coiling completely around his left biceps.

Mike will undergo a bronchial procedure—one of those camera-in-a-tube kind of procedures tomorrow morning. "This could be it," I think he said, not really knowing what he meant. Then the doctor and a posse of young deputies came in and gathered at the foot of the bed, a couple of them in back jostling for position. The doctor pronounced, "We've got some major decisions to make."

I left the room when the nurse came in to find a vein for his IV. His veins were collapsing from relentless poking by a parade of nurses and medical technicians. Jeez, what is this damned thing that creeps in on so many legs, that seems programmed to test a person's capacity for humiliation, that remains so untouched by thousands of doctors and researchers as it takes so many thousands of lives? What the hell is going on?

Now its later and I sit at the coffee house; I find myself wondering if Mike might die tomorrow. I mouth silently something Mike had said: "It's not fair." I follow the statement with a stream of reactions: "It's *not* fair, Mike. It's wrong and you're right. Hang in there! You'll be OK. You'll get through tomorrow and you'll have a good Christmas—at home and with friends."

I sit here writing but, Tom, I just want to go home. God, how I wish the Christmas tree was already up, festooned with lights and foisting cheer on us all—that sweet, quiet cheer that

I've felt from Christmas trees all my life.

Now, on my 40th Christmas, I wonder if that "sweet, quiet cheer" will be enough. Life seems edged with a new sadness. Melancholy invades all my brighter emotions and I wonder, "Are we all dying a little?"

Love,
Chris

A misstep

Reflective, honest criticism is the highest duty we owe our friends . . .

Harriet Beecher Stowe

Dear Chris,

I sent you three days ago a rough draft of the introduction to my *Keeping Spiritually Fit* manuscript. I sought your editing expertise.

I didn't sleep easily the last two nights and now know why. The introduction I sent you was lousy. My goal as a writer is to compose lean yet substantial work. The piece I mailed you was verbose and preachy. When I am unclear in my thoughts, I get wordy. When I am unsure of my message, I become promotional.

I initially felt raw embarrassment with the pathetic, puffy pages resting in your hands. Then I rallied with this thought: our bond is resilient enough for you to tolerate my imperfect creations. You are bright and caring enough to criticize my writing without rejecting my person, a fine line we will be constantly treading as we co-author and co-edit these mutual letters. For partners, a litmus test for the strength of their bond might be wallpapering together; for our friendship, collaborating on this book will furnish ample challenge.

Nonetheless, if this letter gets to you before we talk, read my piece of junk if you wish, then please dump it in the trash. When I have sufficiently licked my self-inflicted wounds, I will give you another introduction—better yet still far, far from perfect.

Such are the exchanges we negotiate in the "city of Friends."

Your friend,
Tom

More to hold on to

Dear Tom,

On our run this week you asked me about Brad, a prominent member of the gay community whose memorial service will
be held next weekend at our church. I talked about him for a
couple of miles, didn't I? We need to talk about our friends and
colleagues who have died and yet, losing so many friends and
colleagues, I wonder if there will ever be enough time in our lives
to do it. I've been thinking of Brad most of the day.

I was very fond of Brad and, hearing that he died, remember thinking that I would have been honored to sing at his service. I'm sure there will be music. Classical, I would guess. Not a
harp. Something crisp—like Brad. Something strong and passionate. Brass, perhaps.

So let me recall how I described Brad to you: forceful,
bright, clever, political. Warm, on occasion, but more often there
was an uptightness about him. He was always a more delightful
conversationalist than he was a good speaker. Like anyone in the
public eye (Brad was someone the TV stations always called when
they needed a reaction from the "gay community"), he had his
detractors. He was prone to political maneuvering and that sometimes cost him allies. I remember his making a risky decision to
back a Republican candidate for mayor. I would guess he had
been attracted to some of the candidate's qualities that he himself
possessed—the candidate was bright, young, ambitious, brash
and he was a maverick. Like Brad, the mayoral candidate always
played the game a little ahead of the field.

Brad was a good coalition builder. He was active, principled,
and ever-mindful of others whether he was hosting a dinner,
holding a fund-raiser, serving on a committee, or settling favors
owed back and forth with his colleagues.

But is any of this accurate? After all, I knew Brad like so
many people did—from a distance. Political clubs, committee
meetings, parties. I'll always remember the few conversations I

did have with him at our local night spots. The noise, the drinks, and the sexual undercurrents all served to lighten our mood and we would talk about politics, art, and other things, but mostly we talked about boyfriends. Boys love to talk about their boyfriends. And in those situations where perfect candor seems called for, the talk coursed with good-natured but genuine urgency. Not so surprisingly, we both had experienced a mix of success and frustration in matters of romance.

For a year or two, I had seen Brad with a beautiful man from Mexico City—magnificent eyes, perfect olive skin, dark hair, and a broad, peaceful face. One evening, fresh from a black-tie dinner and dressed in a tuxedo, Brad reported being frustrated that the relationship had not moved past friendship. I followed with a report that I was trying to keep one of my current relationships firmly in the friendship zone. Reverse romantic entanglements. We laughed but it wasn't lost on Brad that our roles were switched and he seemed just a little annoyed with me.

Some months later, I saw him perched at Flick's. No tuxedo this time and there was a bit of a slouch in his profile. His smile was both warm and wan—which would have put it somewhere in the helpless range. Brad had a very expressive face—one of the important consolations for those of us with large features. We talked for awhile and his mood brightened. Both of us were animated and somewhat flirtatious. At some point, my guard went back up and I brusquely announced that I needed to head home. I retreated into my aloofness—my evening mask of choice—and Brad resumed his harlequin mood. I squared off and extended my arm over his shoulder in a half-hug gesture. He reached up and as my arm and body slid away he caught my elbow, held tight, and then, clasped his hand around my arm, punctuating with squeezes at my elbow, my wrist, and finally my fingers as I pulled away. I was out the door. I thought of our silent, articulating arms off and on for a few days. I think of our arms now with a considerably greater sense of poignancy.

Sometimes missing someone means collecting a bunch of tiny memories and stringing them together, hoping there might be enough of that person to hold on to. I wish I had more. I wish we could have all held on to Brad.

Love,
Chris

After the age of forty

> After the age of forty, there isn't much to live for except friendship.
>
> Francine du Plessix Gray

Dear Chris,

Now that you've turned 40 and I've reached 50, this note seems in order.

I don't buy Gray's dire analysis. There's plenty to live for in my life. Indeed, the older I climb, my reasons for embracing existence have become more varied and numerous.

When I was a youngster, my sphere of concern was essentially limited to myself. As I have matured, my universe has grown to include buddies and parents, then partner and fellow workers, followed by children and congregants. Having passed the half-century mark, Chris, I firmly believe the only realm worth saluting and respecting is the largest one imaginable—the fathomless web of all existence.

That web assuredly includes prized friends.

I covet friends more than ever—not tons but a good few, not fawning but truthful ones, not men *or* women but both. Friends who will caress me across the miles, who will hold me when I falter or grow weary, who will nudge me when my moral muscles are flabby, who will honor the sharing or withholding of my secrets, who need both my casseroles and embraces, who could get along just fine, thank you, without my presence, but choose not to do so.

Good, dear, close friends like that, like you, to travel alongside, down the homestretch.

Your friend,
Tom

Warts, Furballs, and Humors

Back in my twenties (which was in the 1930s) I was keeping a journal, and I wrote in the journal, "I am a lesbian; I must face this truth." Then rereading my journal a few days later, I thought, "Gosh, I shouldn't have that down here in black and white. Someone might read it." So I took my scissors and cut out that sentence and tossed it in the wastepaper basket. Perhaps half an hour later, as I was moving around the room, I glanced down and there, glaring up at me most conspicuously from the wastepaper basket, was this cut-out sentence. And I remember that it hit me: you can't throw truths away. If you try to throw them away, you get into worse trouble than the trouble you were trying to escape.

Barbara Demming

Tom and I have a friendship that is not sexual and yet our friendship has everything to do with sexuality. Or should I say: Tom and I enjoy a friendship that has nothing to do with sexuality but is always sexual. Wait, I'm confused! What I mean is, the personal energies of our friendship include sexual energy even though we would never have genital contact.

Especially since we started writing letters to each other, Tom and I deliberately explore attitudes and topics that we might otherwise conveniently steer clear of. At the center of these topics is our different sexual orientations. But believe me, there are plenty of other differences to talk and write about.

This section of letters, more than any other perhaps, shows us warts and all. We can't always put on our best face with each other and we don't want to do that with you either.

We begin and end this section with letters from Tom that share some of his perspective on sexual orientation and male friendship. As a gay man, I am very proud of the work Tom has done through his writing and in his community service to reverse attitudes of bigotry and discrimination. To achieve full civil rights for gay men and lesbians, we need the clear thinking and heart-felt support of our straight brothers and sisters. Tom has been there for us again and again—marching in Gay Pride Parades, speaking out from the pulpit against homophobia, and bringing gays, straights, and bisexuals together in dance, discussion, and workshops.

His support for gay men and lesbians goes well beyond the obligatory, liberal rhetoric. He understands that sexual expression is at the very center of everyone's life and that all of us, regardless of our sexual orientation, must look deep into our own centers to really appreciate this rich dimension of life.

We aren't neuter!

Dear Chris,

You and I have often talked about sexual orientation. Our conversations and letter writing have helped us separate our convictions from our confusions.

First, most lesbians and gays choose the term "sexual orientation" over "sexual preference" because it means that one is born with an affectional predisposition to gayness. The ensuing job is to confirm what innate sexuality dictates. There are also political benefits as well to using the word "orientation."

And yet we have both pondered the overlooked significance of sexuality's "preference" dynamic. Doesn't a critical moment or series of moments occur when lesbians and gays affirm their true sexual identity, when they say "yes," when they quit trying to act straight and choose to live their sexual being to its most natural and fullest potential? There is a strong, life-affirming dynamic of choice in matters of sexuality.

And this goes for heterosexuals as well. All of us would be far more mature and responsible sexually, if we were intentional and clear about our sexual choices rather than being swept along by the prevailing social conventions. Whether homosexual, heterosexual, or bisexual, we can never take our sexual identity for granted. We must choose it, shape it, update it, embody it. Speaking about changing perspectives on black identity, writer Toni Morrison once remarked in an interview: "Now people choose their identities. Now people choose to be Black." I think that's an authentic, valuable process.

Perhaps the radical lesson for all of us is that our ethical, spiritual, sexual identities are never created or fulfilled by another person, man or woman. We are ultimately sculpted from within.

Second, we acknowledge the blatant double standard when it comes to defending one's sexuality. For example, the causation of homosexuality is investigated relentlessly, but no one ever seriously analyzes the genesis of heterosexuality. The possessors of heterosexist privilege never have to question why, how, and what they do. Heterosexuals are relatively safe from scrutiny.

Third, sexual oppression probably more than any other form of oppression sabotages people right where we live and love. Sexuality is intimately related to spirituality; both go to the core of our personhood. We human beings are simply not neuter. When our sexual choices are declared unnatural, then our very being is wounded, precisely where we cannot bear to have it assaulted.

When our sexual expression is denied, we become devitalized. As lesbian activist and author Demming declares in the title of her book: "we cannot live without our lives." Not to affirm our intrinsic sexuality is to plant seeds of self-destruction.

I experience vast sadness and rage when religious denominations throughout our land declare it's okay to be a gay or lesbian clergyperson as long as you refrain from practicing your sexuality. How demeaning an edict! You can be assured that heterosexuals would rise up in droves if such a cruel judgment were rendered to throttle *our* sexual behavior.

Michael Denneny put it similarly:

> I find my identity as a gay man as basic as any other identity I can lay claim to. Being gay is a more elemental aspect of who I am than my profession, my class, or my race.

Fourth, sexual discrimination is devastating because it undermines the very foundations of an individual's private and public life. We liberals like to say that one's homosexuality is a private matter—"What you do in the bedroom is your own business." But that's a trap well-intentioned people fall into, for the truth is that the private and public domains of our lives cannot be easily compartmentalized. You are a gay man twenty-four hours a day, Chris, and I am a straight man, twenty-four hours a day.

Furthermore, as long as there are written and unwritten laws on our current books which degrade and discriminate against gays and lesbians, then one's sexual identity is most certainly a public matter. As long as you can be fired from jobs, denied an education, made unwelcome in religious families and leadership, then one's private behavior remains of critical public significance. The personal and political are inextricably intertwined in human existence.

Fifth, I find that homophobia and sexual discrimination are devastating precisely because both oppressor and oppressed are dehumanized in the process. Everyone one of us is sabotaged when any one of us attempts to establish sexual superiority by belittling or demonizing the choice of another. Sexual prejudice that degenerates often into terrorism, whether against gays or women, heterosexuals or men, is all of one heinous fabric. Any break in it will finally help us all, even though that break will be seen by some to challenge them severely at the time.

This is a lengthy epistle, Chris, full of views and venting. I only ask that we keep the conversation alive on this panoply of concerns. Who are you? Who am I? We can help one another clarify and deepen our chosen sexual identities and behaviors. We already have.

Your friend,
Tom

Our gay-straight support group

> It is in the integration of gay and straight men in our
> male community that we are coming to know there is
> nothing more powerful than friendship, and no friend-
> ships are more powerful than those which risk the
> experience of honesty and intimacy and love . . .
> The question is not whether we think the same,
> believe in the same God, respond erotically to the
> same sex, but whether we are willing to stand for
> one another.
>
> Kurt Kuhwald

Dear Chris,

You and I have had the privilege of sharing a gay-straight support group over nearly three years. It is one of the cool, restorative spots along my path. And yet, in some people's conversation, our group's experience is lumped together with a variety of male activities derogatorily referred to as "male bonding" exercises.

As men, we are touching and talking with one another in more meaningful ways than our conventional modes of bragging, drinking, and sporting together. I'm all for greater openness and brother-building among men. The more we risk intimacy with other males, the less likely we will do harm to self or neighbor, earth or animals. Yet the phrase "male bonding" bothers me.

"Bonding," itself, denotes cement or servitude or molecular structure. None of these definitions does justice to the intense commitments I see being fashioned among brothers today.

But even more troubling is the sarcastic tone that often accompanies the term as it's bandied about in social gatherings. For example, "Well, I guess the boys are off tonight engaging in some *male bonding*." The term is used to connote being childish, or doing something weird or illicit, certainly clandestine. What the sarcasm also communicates is an attitude that "bonding" is the best that men can do; that more genuine interaction is beyond our capacity.

Additionally, sexist and homophobic realities dominate our culture. Countless examples of sexual terrorism give a justifiably horrendous reference to "male bonding" as well. Campus fraternities talk about protecting the "brotherhood" and fostering "male bonding," often euphemisms for active misogyny, heterosexism, sexual threats, and violent crimes.

I may not be an active co-conspirator or perpetrator in violations against women, but my maleness is dehumanized by association. I may not be directly responsible for male violence, but I am clearly related. That is why, Chris, my most active socio-ethical commitment currently is participating in various local and continental organizations which combat violence against self, against other men, and especially against women and children.

Despite the resurgence of male backlash against women's drive for full equality, despite rampant violence among men, there is a rising, counter revolution among some gay and straight men, who bear daily witness to gender justice and joy. For we know, as Dennis Altman reminds us:

> Those societies that are best able to accept homo-sexuals are also societies that are able to accept assertive women and gentle men, and they tend to be less prone to the violence produced by hypermasculinity.

In creating a world of gender equity and compassion, men are also growing more intimate as brothers. *Bonding* is not a strong enough word to do justice to the enlivening, faithful commitment of men to one another. The better term is *befriending*.

Your friend,
Tom

The most curious creature of all

Dear Tom,

   So, what is going on, Chris, that you want to tell Tom about?

   Well, let me say at the outset that I never stop watching people. And more often than not, my skills of scrutiny and judgment target men in my life. What fascinating creatures! They are my teammates and my competitors. My brothers and my conquerors. In "The Cowboy on a Postcard" I showed one side of my fascination with men. And yet there are many times when my awe falls away (from illusion fatigue?) and I find myself inspecting the motliest of crews!

   Here are some word–sketches, some caricatures that I have scribbled in my journal over the past few months. No one recognizable except for the one soul at the end. I hope you see this as idle mischief on my part. I know you have no natural taste for gossip and maybe that's why I want to pull you into the fray. Imagine scanning a group of men with binoculars and resting your gaze (or mine) upon different specimens. They are unaware, innocent, natural. Here we go.

- The nervous sidekick—deferential and insightful but often in an ingratiating way. Eternally observant yet, at the same time, fading in and out of everyone else's view. Are those binoculars around his neck, too?

- The cheerful insider—promotional on behalf of his companions *and* himself. Que–sera–sera–but–gosh–life–is–so–amazing. Hell–bent on creating a subculture with all the attendant jargon, rituals, secret hugs, and handshakes. And knowing them all better than anyone else.

- The lone warrior—searching for a tribe but prowling just outside the fire circle. Fully respectful of male-to-male situations, knowing that any one of them might constitute a blood brother ceremony.

- The noble hound—taking a stretch and circling his bed of

warm blankets before settling again. Gentle, apologetic, self-effacing.

- The perennial mascot—youngster, character, vagabond, pup. When will he embrace his adult reality?

- The masked man—surely, this one's on the endangered species list. His identity, his intellect, and his heart are all placed "off limits." He interacts with others by offering the perfect summation, the barbed observation, or the cool stare.

- The Adonis/Eunuch—such a beautiful face! How could any sentient being be so oblivious to the admiration and lust being directed his way? Ah, it's a studied disregard for the people around him. What affection or compassion could this one really offer in return?

- I turn the glasses around and find . . . me, the most curious creature of all! Angry, tired, and feeling more burdened than blessed. Reluctantly cheerful and covertly hostile—that is to say, humorous. What do I want from people? Shake me out of it! Talk to me, hug me, make an obscene gesture, get my heart pumping . . . something!

Tom, I sometimes struggle to be present and authentic in my conversation and in my interaction with people. I love them, I hate them, I'm perplexed by them. And I have so many different feelings about myself. My heart, mind, and soul seem to gallop in different directions so much of the time. (And as soon as a fourth horse shows up, I'll likely be drawn, quartered, and left holding the reins.) I embody multiplicity in my life experience. My best hope is to achieve unison or at least harmony, but how can I focus my identity?

When you and I speak, Tom, there is much that is said and much that is left unsaid. When we run through the park, our talk flows differently at seven miles an hour than when we stand or walk. I may regard certain personal experiences as inconsequen-

tial and never mention them and then be torn apart with curiosity as to whether or not you have the same ones. And then I wonder if I'm careless with your identity. The many "Tom's" that I tell
different friends about may actually bear little resemblance to
each other.

I visualize my multiple selves all flowing like distinct humors throughout my body—spit, sweat, blood, tears, semen, and
mucous being the obvious ones. Tom, you and I are different, so
our balance of humors must be different. I am more the icono-
clast. The rejecter. I am often lyrical and humorous. And I am un-
relentingly wary of the status-quo. You build trust. You love
stories and quotes for their value in communicating ideas and
promoting agreement. You're the philatelist and I'm more the car-
nival barker. From where I sit, it's all the greatest show on earth
and everyone plays a part.

Tom, this doesn't seem so much a letter as it does a furball I
just coughed up on your living room carpet. That's all for now.

Love,
Chris

Ever-appearing, ever-vanishing

Dear Tom,

There have been a few times during our friendship where I have been aware of healthy disagreement between us. "Healthy disagreement" doesn't really capture it. "Tension" comes closer. Along with: "amazement, distance, and pleading" as well.

I say healthy because I always feel that our souls point to some common understanding, much like artists work with vanishing points on the horizon to create perspective in their drawings. You and I work with common points, too, though ours are ever-appearing as well as ever-vanishing.

Here is one common point: We share in the struggle to find peace in this swirling cosmos and our place in it. The crux of our journey is discovering whether we are each isolated or all connected. I announced at one of our men's group meetings that I was learning to draw strength from the notion that "no one is alone." More and more, I am feeling that people *are* connected. I am learning that hope is not futile. Indeed, hopelessness and isolation are the myth.

"How do you know that? How can you be sure?" you asked.

A quick aside: sometimes your rhythm of speech enthralls me, Tom. I feel very close to who you are. I think that I truly see you and know that I really care about this person I see. Being close to someone requires seeing that person as precious, as fragile, as breakable, as bleedable. You are all these things in my eyes and much more.

Anyway, you wondered how I knew that "no one is alone." You were intrigued by the freshness of my statement of faith and you needed me to expand on my feelings, perhaps as a way of reaffirming a tenet of your own personal theology. My answer could hardly have satisfied—more stumbling than substance. I only knew that the notion of connectedness—which has now grown to become a cornerstone of my life—gives me strength and a position to grow from and to build on. No one has to be an orphan in this world.

On another occasion, we discussed the unique relationship that can develop between brothers—biological or social. You held that, between father and son, a "brother" relationship couldn't be realized.

"I think it can," I said softly, not wanting to slow your passionate case for brotherhood but wanting to enter a small footnote of disagreement.

A moment later you turned to me on the couch and asked—with the same urgent appeal I remembered from an earlier conversation—"What do you mean, Chris? Why do you think you can be as close with your father?"

In a household with five boys, Dad more often seemed like one of the boys. He did not project himself as a man of towering, unapproachable strength. Furthermore, I have always felt we have a similar litany of attributes: affable, intelligent, caring, verbal, and musical. Our birthdays are only six days apart so even the zodiac aligns with our similarities. Now, in our adult years, we seem to balance each other with envies: I envy his having a family; he envies my comfort with singing and performance. In our case, I feel the father/son roles *are* surmountable. Our friendship and our feelings of brotherhood continue to grow.

So, yes. I can be as close to Dad as I can be to a brother. There are challenges in being close to a brother, as well. I often wonder about my own fraternal relationships. There are five boys in our family and we have no sisters. We boys speak the same language and sprinkle in most of the same idioms. We laugh in a similar manner—a little loud and a little too quick. We share many of the same habits and same opinions. Let me risk for a moment and expound on this collective creature, the Hassett Boy:

- We're smarter than everyone else in the room.

- We know what's best for us, for you, and for the whole world generally.

- We love music and laughter and we can cheer up the town grump with ease.

- We listen just long enough to hear the reading of the rules and then we play hard.

- We have appetites that sometimes get the best of us.

- We care about people who are down and out, who are old, who are poor.

- We have limited attention spans.

- We love people who laugh heartily, who are agile in spirit, and who like us. In fact, everyone *must* like us. It's no wonder that we try so hard to be liked. It's our survival.

- We can also be cruel in our judgment. We have let some people fall into the abyss of our disapproval—sometimes for no apparent reason, sometimes for many reasons. People who remain blasé about us are a great puzzle. We strain to knock people off their indifference toward us. It's unbelievable that people might choose to ignore us.

What are the unseen rules that control our lives? Why don't I grab the box that this game arrived in and investigate or even change the rules so long ago internalized. The rule-monger can be oblivious to the guiding principles of life, the nurturing forces beyond the rules. We live out our lusts and ignore our true, life-giving passions.

Tom, I commit myself to a new balance, a life-affirming balance. More later.

Love,
Chris

Prejudice can cut both ways

Dear Chris,

As a white, heterosexual, upper middle-class male I receive my share of roasting and ridicule, both for my own sins and for those of my associates and ancestors. The damages of institutional racism, sexism, and homophobic discrimination continue unabated as long as my cohorts and I, in places of authority, fail to repent, fail to resist further injustices, fail to reconstitute society by sharing power and resources.

Yet I also experience personal hurt, whenever I am the butt of discrimination and revenge, intentional or unintentional. The prejudice is not as severe or systemic, but the cut draws blood just the same.

A mutual acquaintance who jogs with the gay-lesbian group called "Front Runners" once said to me: "Tom, you live near the Park, why don't you run with us some Saturday morning?" He paused, then continued, "but, I guess, you wouldn't want to be known as one who runs around with faggots, would you?"

He meant it primarily in jest, but there was a cutting tone in his voice. His joke slashed. I've never been honest enough to tell our friend that he hurt me with his words. Whether or not I ever run with the "Front Runners" (and I probably never will feel sufficiently comfortable doing so) isn't the real point; my integrity is. I need to be safe and caring enough with my gay friends and acquaintances to confront your provincialism or prejudice whenever it rears its ugly head. Otherwise, we lapse into a state of sweetness and light, failing to venture the truthfulness required of authentic kinship.

Another example. AIDS has brought straights and gays closer together in multiple ways, as we labor alongside one another to assault this deadly plague. AIDS has also spawned occasions for gays and straights to attack one another.

At our AIDS Project board meetings, we heterosexual members have been regularly and roundly criticized for never fully empathizing with gay patients. Then when we try to be bridges, we get walked on by warring gay factions. We can't win. Sometimes I want, in the worst way, to blurt out: "Friends, we need, every one of us, to beat this vicious, deadly virus. I cannot enter your suffering or bear the brunt of your torturous agony, but I do care. Some straights agonize too."

I was asked recently, by non–members, to do Jack's memorial service after he died of AIDS. This is an increasingly common request which our congregation willingly meets. But this particular service was overflowing with hostility, most of it aimed directly against religion and heterosexist society. Deserved as much of it was and is, I still wanted, late in the onslaught, to rise and firmly say: "Stop, comrades. This is a religious community, and flawed as it is, our church welcomes and loves you, living or dying, and we are doing our damnedest to heal and console one another amid this unspeakable tragedy. We can ill afford to chew one another up with venom and vitriol. I urge you to fight the disease, not this faith and not your friends . . . we remain kin to the end."

Someday soon, I hope to be brave enough not only to *think* these thoughts but to *voice* them. "Easy" is never another word for religion or friendship or anything that truly matters, is it?

Your friend,
Tom

That tricky course

Dear Tom,

I often think of our morning runs. Though they only come once a week, they currently comprise my entire fitness program. In the past, I've been a fitness freak but now I seem to have greatly relaxed that tendency.

Remember the psychiatrist some years back when the running boom was young? He prescribed running for his patients and found that their functionality on all levels vastly improved. Maybe we should invite some of the park residents to join us on our morning runs.

It's an attractive though problematic idea. My fears quickly surface: We invite one person to join us and confront the first obstacle—he doesn't have shoes. "Run with us for a week and I'll buy you some shoes," I offer. "You go too fast," he counters. "We'll run your speed for awhile. And we'll go a little further each day." Et cetera.

Anyway, all this tugging and pulling. His wanting to run but scared of the change. Our wanting him to run with us but scared of the burden we'd be creating for ourselves. All of us projecting our fears out into the world.

When we run, we do it one step at a time. When we care about people, we have to do it moment to moment.

You might imagine the folk-hero potential in all of this. After a few months, dozens of homeless people are running in the morning. Their lives begin to change. They get jobs, places to live, people in their lives they care about and who care about them. And now I'm projecting my hopes. Both hopes and fears take us away from the fundamental act of caring.

What was my immediate thought when I passed one of our brothers earlier today?

"Run with us. I don't want to see you cold, hungry, and alone, wrapped in that old blanket. Maybe you wish you were awake enough to ask us for something. Maybe you hate us as we trot past you in our clean shorts and expensive shoes. Maybe you just feel cold, hungry, and alone. I don't like to feel that way. In fact, I'd carry it off with very little dignity indeed."

So, will I invite some silent form to rise and join us? Probably not. But Tom, I have to tell you, I'd want someone to do that for me. When I've been discouraged and depressed, I've had advocates. These people need advocates, too. Who will be their advocates? If I tried to help, really help, would I find my energies drained? Would I become a cold and lonely form? Is that my real fear?

Caring is that tricky course that steers between unrealistic hopes and paralyzing fears. I have yet to find a caring path in much of my life. I lack the courage to emerge from the shadows on this and so many problems. I remain an aspiring, frustrated creature.

Love,
Chris

Forgive me

Forgiveness is the final form of love.

Reinhold Niehbuhr

Dear Chris,

It is painful to face ourselves when we are acting in exclu-
sionary or degrading fashion, but it is more agonizing, over the
long haul, when we ignore or suppress personal wrongdoing.

A few years back I preached a sermon on "Staying Together"
which dwelt on committed partnerships. It focused exclusively on
heterosexual marriage. There were reasons for this (no excuses,
simply explanations); my main one being that while previously I
had spoken about committed relationships in general, I wanted
this time to center on what I knew best—explicating some bittersweet learnings from my own marriage with Carolyn.

I goofed. I was blatantly heterosexist. I left out any mention,
disclaimer, or translation, with respect to lesbian and gay partnerships. I can't even claim that it was unintentional. I knew better.
Commitment was the operative concept in my talk, but I didn't so
much as tip my hat to those of you in our congregation wrestling
with durable devotion in the gay, lesbian, or bisexual worlds.

Several of you felt affronted, discounted. You wrote me
forthright, critical letters ("We are a gentle, angry people . . . " goes
the song), phoned me, even visited me. A full-fledged "lover's
quarrel" broke out, blossoming into a powerful two-plus hour
evening conversation with Carolyn and me—all of us exchanging
heartfelt comments on love, commitment, partnership, marriage,
and much more. Over 65 lesbians, gays, and bisexuals, along with
a dozen straights came primed to speak, listen, and grow. It shook
our foundations, rattled some windows, even led to dismantling
portions of our relational house. Since then, we have been building together a sturdier structure of respect and affection.

You yourself, Chris, called early on and upbraided me. I

remember being defensive, but your call was necessary for me, for us. If our friendship is to endure difficult, awkward times, then we must be willing to define and share our hurts, allow healing, that we might more honestly embrace later on.

Your friend,
Tom

To stretch

Dear Tom,

We spoke of balance this morning. I was beginning to understand that muscle balance may offer a partial explanation for some lower-back pain I've been having. Thanks for passing on the name of your chiropractor. I'll make an appointment this week.

Also, we both agreed that stretching exercises would help. Stretching is a wonderful activity—too often ignored in all aspects of our lives. Regular stretching guarantees our capacity to move and flow. To change. To expand.

I recalled an exchange I recently had with a new friend, Michael, about performing: "It may be that you need to stretch in a new direction, Chris." His applying a physical act to the intangible seemed to make so much sense. I could visualize how fresh artistic expression might reshape me and draw forth new energies.

Stretching has so often been a metaphor for changes in my life. When Michael asked how he could help me, I responded, "Help me take out the kinks and the knots. Help me find what I yearn to express. Help me stretch. Tell me when I'm 'warm.' Help me identify what my feelings are in that half-second before I suppress them."

Talking to you, Tom, we agreed that if we aren't capable of expanding and stretching, then how could we use energy for growth when it does come? We have to be limber.

So I wonder, am I limber now? Do I feel clarity in my life right now? When did I last experience clarity? Balance?

I recall sitting with a group and, with eyes shut, being guided through a meditation . . .

> Following directions from a soft-voiced woman, I choose a favorite landscape and picture myself there—a quiet beach on a sunny, warm day. I am informed by the voice that I have a buried treasure there at the beach and I'm asked to uncover it. I see before me a rosewood and cherry box, simple and finely crafted with brass corners.

Inside are dozens—or an infinity—of stages and performance spaces. They reveal themselves one after the other, miniaturized and complete with props, scenery, actors, costumes, dancing. Like a tiny toy store coming alive but the stories are not childish. They are important, powerful, and I long to lose myself, to find myself in the swirling realities before me.

I stretch to make my life a permanent home for this liberating vision of endless possibility.

Love,
Chris

Nonsexual friendship

Dear Chris,

Men are told that one of the reasons we fail at befriending other men is our fear of intimacy; specifically, our pervasive homophobia—anxiety about being physically, perhaps sexually, close with other men. Therefore, we remain at a distance, engaging in activities together, occasionally sharing heart-talk, but generally staying out of touch.

The more I grow ties with gay men, the more I realize that the opposite truth holds for me: namely, it is freeing to have a nonsexual friend, someone where the sexual energy, games, and ploys are essentially at bay. I choose to be a monogamous partner, so I am neither interested in nor available for sexual involvement beyond my marriage. Yet sexual attraction awakens, lurks in the atmosphere, whenever I interact with women. This is not the case for me with men. I may find them physically handsome and emotionally vibrant, but I am not moved sexually.

Therefore, when I, a straight man, and you, Chris, a gay man, are respectful of our distinct sexual identities and yearnings, allowing each other to be who he is, we can relate freely and fully. I appreciate the way David Michaelis phrases it:

> I can't imagine going through life and not having someone like Mike. I don't know what those people who don't have a friend like Mike do. I almost find it hard to believe that everybody doesn't. I mean you gotta have somebody. And I mean a nonsexual friend. There's only so much that you'll tell your whomever, and at that point you need the kind of guy with whom you can just really be yourself. That's the purest kind of relationship. There's nothing asked, nothing expected, nothing to cloud it up. I accept him as he accepts me.

The poet Galway Kinnell once penned something both mystifying yet revealing about friendship: "the body makes love possible." I fully acknowledge the role the body plays even in nonsexual ties. Friends are not disembodied realities, after all. We are corporeal not ethereal.

There is a range of life-affirming ways in which our bodies can connect as gay and straight men. Our bodies are deeply connected, Chris, without being joined, when we run together, hug, back-slap or butt-thump, even sing together. Our bodies are integral to our separate beings as well as to our friendship. In sum, our friendship, while physical, is not sexual.

Once we straight and gay men diminish our fears and progress toward heightened trust, we can relate erotically without acting sexually. What a relief! We can touch, be in sensual alignment, but have no underlying anxiety about pursuit or romance. We can focus on the social, spiritual, and intellectual dimensions of our companionship.

All of this highlights the wisdom of what Roman Catholic leaders have been saying about celibacy. They have long contended, and rightly so, that celibacy, at its richest, is more than abstinence from sexuality. Celibacy frees us from the possessive, exclusive, dependent entanglements of a sexual liaison.

The words "friend" and "free" grow etymologically and existentially out of each other. The old English word *freo* meant free; not in bondage, noble, glad. The old English word *freon* meant to love, and the word *freond* becomes our modern English "friend."

As friends, at our finest, we leave one another with our freedom intact.

Your friend,
Tom

Sexual Odysseys

Tom and I have exchanged a series of letters examining our sexual and emotional development. Whereas Tom managed to explicate the important passages of his sexual odyssey in a couple of letters, I took considerably more ink and paper to identify some of the themes and lessons in my development. Tom just couldn't believe how the letters kept coming! And maybe I was a little surprised, too. But the story seemed to have a need all its own to be told. So I hung in there with it right up to the present.

We continue to joke and jab about our different experiences and our different handling of the subject in writing. We acknowledge that Tom's sex life has been more uniform and less eventful than mine—though there were many times when I would have settled for less variety and fewer events.

We also wonder how much of the difference—in both our experience and our willingness to reveal—might be explained by sexual orientation. I do believe that gay men talk more openly with each other about their sexual experiences and, in writing these letters to Tom, I tried to achieve that same level of sharing.

Once again, I firmly believe that our distinctness—as men, as sexual beings, and as writers—is only partially explained by sexual orientation. As we allow our conversation and writing to deepen, we are more aware of our underlying commonality. Although the details of our life and experience serve as an important vehicle for sharing, I think that friends eventually reach a plane of understanding that transcends the particular.

In sharing this set of letters with you, we hope that we have managed to keep our focus more on self-discovery than on self-centeredness, more on growth than on escapade. In short, we hope you hear more rings than thuds.

A child of my time

Dear Chris,

I can best launch our heart-to-heart sharing with a summary of my odyssey as a straight man in response to the gay experience. Three dominant memories come to mind.

Thirty-five years after I first knew him I realize that red-haired Michael who lived just down the hill from our family was gay. There was a bounce in his gait and a twinkle in his eyes when he cavorted with us boys in the sandlots after school.

No one talked about homosexuality back in the '50s and certainly not in our sleepy, conservative village, but Michael was different from most of the guys on the block. He knew it, we knew it, and none of us knew quite what to do with it. Including Michael. Especially Michael. He squirmed, then bristled, amid the gender expectations and pressures of our era. He never seemed comfortable with his sexual identity. How could he? We didn't let him. So he felt strange, grew estranged, left town. I later learned that he had taken his life.

Michael was a casualty of his time. My time. Your time. All time.

Seeing my high school chum Maxine secretly necking with Cathy, an adult woman who managed the local drugstore, in our nearby park late one evening threw me a floating curve. While their behavior seemed unusual, even weird, to me, their nuzzling was actually no clumsier than what we "normal" boys and girls were managing in the back seats of our cars. In the same park.

I was so inexperienced and frantic in negotiating my own erotic moves that I had little cause to worry about how others might be romancing differently.

Then there is my second cousin, Ramon, who always came to our family reunions alone or with a new male roommate. Back then, I naively assumed you acquired an adult roommate once in your lifetime, and you got him during your frosh year at college.

Anyway, we children were enthralled by Ramon's luxuriant hair and the magical puppets with which he mesmerized our entire clan after dinner. His poodles were something special too.

I felt a poignant sadness when he no longer appeared at family gatherings. His absence left a gaping hole. There was no one quite like him in our rather staid, provincial clan. One of our relatives off-handedly remarked that Ramon just didn't seem to fit into our family. He seemed fine to me, a nice fit, and far more interesting than that particular kinsman. I never saw Ramon again until two decades later at my father's memorial service. He was as magical as ever.

You see, Chris, I was a child of a locale and era where straight, white maleness was the predominant ethos. With few exceptions, women were second-class creatures, people of color worked for, not beside, you, and homosexuality was mentioned only in crude, demeaning barbs in the locker-rooms of one's adolescence.

My conventional upbringing was a typical American scenario with its smattering of Michaels, Maxines, and Ramons.

I grew into adulthood and prepared for the ministry. During my seminary career, I was given field work in Sausalito, California, a community filled with gay bars. One of my early assignments was to visit local pubs and make sociological observations for class analysis, and, if lucky, win a convert or two for the neighborhood Presbyterian church.

In retrospect, it was a condescending, futile mission. We progressive seminarians liked to talk about "their" behavior as being variant rather than deviant, but our homophobic gawking was thinly disguised arrogance. We treated gays and lesbians as oddities to be tolerated, projects to be studied. I am ashamed that I even got class credit for these denigrating forays into a scene about which I knew little, didn't belong, hardly cared. Yes, Chris, I was a child of my time—1965.

Things started to get more personal. In 1972, a high-ranking member of our Pasadena, California congregation walked up to me at the back of the social hall during a packed-house performance of *Jesus Christ Superstar*, the stirring rock musical. When Mary Magdalene (or was it Judas Iscariot?) started to sing, "I Don't Know How to Love Him," my friend, Don, clandestinely drew close, slipped his hand into mine, and held tight for several moments.

Perhaps I should have read it as a romantic overture, but I didn't. These were "touchy-feely" times, so Don's gesture didn't strike me as anything other than warm and affectionate, if a bit unusual.

Weeks went by. He began to show up at an increasing number of my workshops and committee meetings. His eyes would wander over my way during the course of the evening. Since I wasn't emotionally available for his signals, they flew right by.

A year or so passed. He and his wife invited me and mine over for a summer's end dinner. Shortly after the meal I went to the bathroom and hot upon my tracks, much to my amazement, was Don. He sneaked into the bathroom with me, then quickly and fervently declared his erotic intentions. Whenever and however, he wanted sex with me. He began to reel off the acts he would like and how proficiently he could perform them. He assured me I would enjoy them too.

I jumped back, shocked, but managed to stammer an unmistakable "No, no thanks, Don! I like you, but I'm not interested in sex with you."

Don wanted me in a way I didn't want him. He felt spurned, an unrequited lover. All I ever wanted with Don was a modest friendship. We parted that night, never comfortable with one another again.

Jump ahead to 1975. Edward rushed up after a worship service in Davenport, Iowa and chewed me out right there on the chancel: "Damn it, Tom, your sermons have dealt with most every imaginable social oppression except the one I suffer daily. I challenge you to dig deep into your conscience and dare to speak sometime about homosexuality and homophobia—then launch a gay–straight dialogue in the Quad Cities, starting right here in our church. I'll match your bravery with my own. Let's come out of our respective closets together and do something truly religious, even revolutionary, for folks in the cornfields!"

Well, Edward was persuasive and I was converted, slowly but surely. As the Zen Buddhists say: "When you are ready, your roshi will appear." Edward was the first of many teachers, in various guises, who have since graced my life on the matter of crashing barriers and constructing bridges between gay and straight men.

Edward and I started a scathingly honest dialogue process which I have continued for twenty years, confronting fears and fostering trust across sexual orientation lines. It has been a process full of mutual awkwardness, anger, and acceptance. Yet once Edward launched me, for better or for worse, I have seldom strayed from the path.

I got involved in the Quad Cities on a broader community basis as well. I conducted many gay and lesbian services of union, although at that juncture, they were all performed off church premises. Neither couples nor I were ready to force issues with my "liberal" church. In celebrating same-sex ceremonies ever since, I have grown to appreciate the utter preciousness of enduring love—wherever, however, and whenever it is incarnated by us humans. Without the supportive context of marital conventions, committed lesbian and gay partnerships have transported my ministry into depths of sadness and sweetness beyond articulation.

Since moving to San Diego in 1978, I have matured in three primary ways with respect to building gay–straight bonds. First, I am more cognizant of and usually more willing to confront my "liberal" phobias concerning gay men, lesbians, and bisexuals. However, some fears are sneaky, pernicious, and difficult to ferret out, let alone face.

Second, the most nurturing support group I've enjoyed in the last decade has been our intentionally balanced cluster of eight gay and straight men. We meet regularly, reveal deeply, and care ongoingly about one another. Members have dropped out, even died, but we have continued to forge unassailable loyalties. Our conversations are deep and healing, precisely because no conversions are attempted to change anyone's attitudes or behavior.

Finally, my friendship with you, Chris, has been one of the unspeakable blessings of our pilgrimage west from Iowa to California. Ours has been what a lesbian colleague calls "revolutionary friendship."

The word "revolution" comes from the Latin meaning "to roll back, to unroll." That's what we embody in our evolving friendship: rolling back the assumptions, biases, backgrounds and tyrannies that keep us humans apart, specifically men apart, more particularly gays and straights apart.

Then, opening up our hearts and minds, we unroll our selves to one another, sharing the joys, missions, lulls, and impasses of being genuine buddies.

Rolling back the negatives so that positives might be unrolled is the rhythm of revolution.

We are practicing revolutionaries.

Your friend,
Tom

Coming out, for me

Dear Tom,

Coming out for me has been a relatively smooth experience. All the gnashing of teeth and anguish leading up to it were far worse. Like most people who have had to face a strong inner reality and reconcile that with the world outside, I have felt "born again." Do you think some of our reactionary-right brothers will take offense?

Growing up, our family engaged in almost constant physical and mental activity. But relatively little discussion about sexuality. There was adequate sex education. From an early age, I always felt I had the facts. In my teen years, I was fascinated and perplexed by brothers and friends as they ventured into the realm of sexuality. I strained to fathom its form and dimensions from their new behavior—an electric restlessness, a continual need for freshly pressed white shirts and hair cream, and new slang spoken with newly deepened voices. What was it all about? What was so compelling about this energy they felt? What was the payoff? What was the point? I watched—from a safe distance—in total fascination.

I perceived my mission to be a friend to everyone in the family. Being the third of five boys, I was uniquely positioned (and dispositioned) to carry out that role. I would befriend each brother and help Mom and Dad keep everything together. Kind of the parent-in-training. In fact, my affiliation with parents was often stronger than with my brothers.

I mentioned my own coming out at the beginning of this letter, commenting on its smoothness. First I came out to myself—which was a far more harrowing and turbulent experience—and then took several years to gather the personal resources and self-acceptance so that I could come out to my family. I had evolved into someone I wasn't sure my parents were willing to accept. I had strayed so far from the role I had assumed as a child—as the parent-in-training.

Within a few hours of receiving "the letter," Mom and Dad

called, their voices trembling with emotion, to say they loved me. A day later we all sat in my living room and covered more territory of the heart than we had in the previous five years. And not just the heart. We spoke honestly about responsible love–making and safe sex though I don't think the term had even been coined yet.

Our relationship leaped to a higher level that day and its further growth has accelerated in ways that I couldn't have imagined. Childhood awkwardness aside, I clearly am blessed with loving, adaptable, caring parents and my appreciation runs deep, wide channels throughout my being. I'm equally grateful for the friendships with my brothers and their families.

Time to move on from these musings. I don't want to be too introspective. I would like "introspective" to mature into "insightful." Thanks for listening. There are more installments ahead, don't you know?

Love,
Chris

Confessions of a recovering homophobic

> Homosexuality is defined by whom we love;
> homophobia is defined by whom we fear and hate.
> Now I ask you: who is healthy and who is sick?
>
> Anonymous

> Homophobia is the disease, not homosexuality.
>
> Robert Wheatley

> Just as the black problem turned out to be a problem
> of white racism, just as the woman problem turned out
> to be one of male sexism, so the homosexual problem
> is really the homophobia of many heterosexuals who
> won't grant God the right to a more pluralistic cre-
> ation.
>
> William Sloane Coffin

Dear Chris,

Before I launch into a listing of some of the subtle homophobias we well-intentioned, liberal straights display, I want to
define the terms involved.

Homophobia literally means "fear of the same," but actually
the disease occurs when we fear a way of life, a same-sex orientation, other than our own as the ruling culture of heterosexuals. So
we really should be talking about "heterophobia," fear of difference, or "homophilephobia," fear of those who love one another. It
is also true that some gays mock the straight world; some lesbians
despise men in general; and that misogyny is rife among both gay
and straight men.

Nonetheless, our society is compulsively heterosexual;
therefore, heterosexism is the practice of individual and institu-

tional discrimination toward gays and lesbians. The laws perpetuate such oppression. Social mores and religious doctrines reinforce the status quo.

To make things worse, gays occasionally buy into the pervasive homophobia of modern society, so you are susceptible to self-loathing. Many gays and lesbians have woefully confessed this fact to me.

But the oppression I am most concerned about, Chris, is the version I and other progressive straights are prone to commit. A gay friend of mine rightly points out that we heterosexuals are no more free of homophobia than we are cleansed of racism or sexism or classism. We merely display differing degrees and levels of intensity in our homophobic reactions depending upon our visceral ease or unease with same-sex behavior. But we are never free of the malaise. We can count on some situation, somewhere, sometime pushing our homophobic button. Since most of us liberals are not suffering from blatant, advanced cases of homophobia, our prejudice is more insidious to spot, then tougher to eradicate.

Here are some of the more prevalent homophobias to which we "liberated" progressives fall prey:

1) A Messiah Complex

The gay community, due to its oppression, is identified by do-gooding heterosexuals as ripe for emancipation. We intervene to free, or at least aid, our ostensibly "powerless" gay sisters and brothers.

Unfortunately, in so doing we perceive gays as a cause not as persons, a beleaguered group rather than capable individuals. As rescuers, we can't help but telegraph haughtiness, practice condescension, perpetuate victimization. We depersonalize and categorize. We display homophobia.

2) We–They

We heterosexuals often feel that we have done our job of supporting gays when we allow outside groups to enjoy our facilities. This is a common pitfall in church circles. It allows us to see the struggle as happening "out there," with others, rather than forcing us to face our own homophobia as well as sexual authenticity. The fact is that issues of sexual orientation are not simply gay issues but straight issues as well. They are human issues.

Furthermore, in gay–straight dialogues we often "do research" on one another rather than creating the climate and conditions for mutual friendship. We straights are inordinately curious about gay behavior, so we fixate the conversation at that level, instead of revealing our own fears and desires about sexual expression. Or we fail to listen to and learn from gay men who are seasoned initiates in the erotic male mysteries.

3) The Blurring Syndrome

We liberals minimize genuine differences between straights and gays by declaring from the outset that we are all human beings anyway. We may share the same ocean, but gays and straights are hardly in the same boat.

There is an Ashley Brilliant cartoon which reads: "You and I are both exactly alike, but there the resemblance ends." Of course, you and I, Chris, have more in common as humans than not, yet our peculiar places of struggle and achievement, yearning and pain need to be articulated if we are to maximize our companionship.

4) From Civil Rights to Identity

Open-minded heterosexuals like to believe that homosexuals are only interested in achieving their legal rights, because, after all, that's something those of us in seats of institutional power can withhold or deliver. The truth is that gays are increasingly, and understandably so, talking more about lifestyle and culture. In so doing, you are becoming more visible and outspoken, often confrontive, which generates unease in the tolerance capacity of the governing class of straights.

For co–equality of power to transpire in American society between persons of variant erotic orientations, it will require radical changes, which, in turn, will cause substantial discomfort and significant anguish for us heterosexuals. Giving up power, stature, and authority is seldom done without a struggle—a fierce and protracted one.

We heterosexuals feel safer when you gays, Chris, battle for civil rights in Washington, D.C. rather than incarnate your budding identities in the streets and work places of our hometowns. Such assertiveness is labeled "flaunting," the term we use when another's behavior unnerves us or cannot be controlled.

5) Pseudo-Acceptance

At the surface level we exude intellectual tolerance of gays. We may even become ingratiating, bending over backwards to be understanding. We accommodate. Sometimes, we straights even assume the thoughts and feelings of gays while submerging our own. This deadens dialogue, since there is no healthy push-and-pull when heterosexuals cloy and comply, pacifying everyone into false serenity.

I sensed this happening, Chris, a few weeks ago in our gay-straight support group when one of the straights romanticized gays as being more giving, open, and tender persons than straights. His description was so idealistic, even gooey, that it didn't resemble any humanity the rest of us knew, gay or straight. Yet, wanting to please, we let it pass.

Blacks and whites, women and men, parents and youth are masters at this game of pseudo-acceptance. In such well-intentioned displays of phoniness, we avoid acknowledging, let alone sharing, our deeper resentments, fears, urges.

Perhaps underlying such superficial acceptance is the scare that in opening up to one another, we straights might lose control of ourselves, maybe clobber gays, or, worse yet, be drawn to one another erotically.

In Alcoholics Anonymous they say: "I'm Jack, and I'm a recovering alcoholic." So, I say to you, Chris: "I'm Tom, and I'm a recovering homophobic. I still fear, distrust, and judge lesbians and gays sometimes as well as respect and befriend you. Plus I have been known to romanticize homosexuals. So my record is checkered. I cannot wish or pray ambivalences away. I am a recovering homophobic."

Your friend,
Tom

The companions of love

Dear Tom,

I'm fascinated by the several forms of subtle homophobia you enumerated in your last letter. I'm a firm believer that most of the barriers between people are arbitrary and dangerous. It's too convenient to hide behind cultural differences, racial differences, religious differences, and sexual orientation differences instead of facing up to the important task of overcoming those differences.

Sometimes we strain to empathize with someone and we hit a brick wall. Sometimes it's ours, sometimes theirs. Sometimes, just a brick wall. There's one wall I really find discouraging because it seems an unfair contrivance, an unnerving dismissal.

"You can't understand," we're told. "You have no idea. You are part of the problem. You are partners with a system that inflicts an unspeakable pain on us."

We reel back, our liberal sensibilities wounded, and we scramble frantically to close the gap—sometimes at our own expense. "I want to understand," we respond. Maybe we go further: "I'll renounce who I am and dedicate my life as an outsider to understanding your unknowable pain." I wonder if you sometimes feel this dynamic when you reach out to different people in your ministry.

If our story needs to be told, then we need all of our listeners' humanness and that includes what is different as well. If I want you, a straight man, to know me, I can't expect you to be gay to understand. Nor can I assume that, if you were gay, you would *automatically* understand. Diversity abounds. But our underlying humanness is always there to be discovered and affirmed. Differentness, like a deep chasm too wide to leap over, represents an opportunity for building a bridge. If we let the edge of the chasm define the edge of our world, we cut ourself off from our own potential, we limit our own reality.

Tom, people *can* build bridges if as a starting point they affirm each other's humanness and build from there. Admittedly, you and I have a lot of common ground already. Bridging for us may be a far easier exercise than for most but it should never be taken for granted.

So here goes: another story about who I am, where I find myself, and how I got here.

In the first years after a person comes out, through a process of self exploration and self-questioning ("What *caused* my gayness?"), gay men and lesbians do in fact look for early patterns and situations that may have shaped their sexuality. I've done this too. What I've realized is that causation happened outside of my own lifetime. It seems to be a gift of the deepest human dimensions, though it didn't arrive fully developed. Indeed, I can see how my orientation has been continually shaped by life experiences and behaviors. I know this exploration cannot unfold and conclude in a single letter. I will write a series of letters with, I hope, a consistent perspective. A several-part exercise in advocacy journalism. It would be a little preposterous to feign objectivity, don't you think? Ah yes, the story.

I'd like to focus on events, involving my early sexual expression. Though arising naturally from limbs and flesh, from curiosity and wonder, the actual expression may have seemed inappropriate in a straight context and be thwarted or even punished. That's not unique to gay development. Our society has a hard time with sexual development generally.

Growing up, my sexual expression was often self-thwarted because I learned early on what was and was not appropriate. Losing approval, especially parental approval, for even a quarter-hour was unbearable. I had to be loved and so I could never compromise my lovability. Like a lot of gay men, I signed on as my own oppressor, trusting no one else with the task. Are we more sensitive, too, as gay people?

The sensual and sexual encounters I did manage in my adolescence were hidden—nearly from myself. Moments on the run. Even I was half-appalled and incredulous.

I remember playing soldiers with Jerry one day when I was about ten. We pretended to be shot and fell off a low wall, grabbing each other as we tumbled onto the grass. Crying in mock anguish and emitting that great, explosive artillery sound that only little boys are capable of, we rolled over and over each other on the lawn. We pressed against each other with mutual urgency—as though we had to feel each other, completely. And despite our heavy winter clothes, I felt naked in his embrace. Imagined intimacy would become my standard practice for years to come.

Another memory finds me pulling my shorts halfway down my butt one day while playing with Robert. In spite of my exhibitionism, my exposure was successfully ignored. Rather than feeling excitement or shared discovery, I harbored feelings of shame and self-deception over this incident. A shiver of guilt ripples down my back even now as I recall it. Consider the crime: I pretended a naiveté while I practiced adolescent lechery. Ambivalence outdistanced any positive feelings or excitement I might have experienced in this situation or others like it. Soon, such displays would become manifest only in my thoughts—thoughts that still had the power to trigger feelings of shame and self-deception. Any greater risk terrified me.

I recall making out for the first time a few years later with Maria. Even more vividly, I think about the two boys who clamored for her attention, who seemed lasciviously inseparable, and who taunted me mercilessly. What a crush I had on both of them! Only summertime in a child's life is big enough to hold some of the dramas we construct. Well into adulthood, I still seem to construct tangled webs of interpersonal affection—involving several people. The more indirect and tangled a situation, the more likely to elicit my response.

From these early experiences—and so many more—confusion and masquerade became two more companions of love.

I craved affection and worked hard to achieve it. Doubly hard to make sure the achievement appeared effortless. But my genius was in the early stages, the entrapment. Sustaining the affection went beyond my talents and, frankly, I didn't see the point. There inevitably came a point of departure. My task was complete. "Bring the maintenance team in," I seemed to say. "What's my next assignment?"

On the other hand, I wonder what my actual motivation could have been? I had to endure the difficult falling outs, the misunderstandings, the anger. What reward did I garner that could eclipse all that unpleasantness? Why did I endear myself to others—men and women—just to have that moment of profound disappointment and whatever reactions followed?

I knew what it was to travel with the circus. I knew about the strain of raising the big top and training the elephants. I mastered the make-up and the costume that could transform the kitchen girl into the beauty astride the white horse. I knew the thrill of the crowd and the rage in the tiger's heart as it suffered the whip. And I also knew the circus would always leave town and I would go with it.

Do you mind if I slip into something less comfortable? Say, the present? Why can't I deliver on the implicit promise of sustained affection? Why do I withhold? Why do I replay the game? Do I think that it will change? Do I need love so desperately that I'll continually endure the pain of not being able to return it? Has impotence of the heart also become a companion of love for me?

So, Tom, this first phase of bridge-building seems to be an assessment of a chasm not between us but one that I hold within.

Is that the lesson? In promoting understanding with other people—whether it reaches across racial lines or across barriers of sexual orientation—we are required to confront our own discontinuities of spirit, our own incongruities of personal philosophy, our own chronicle of awkward acts. Like the old adage says: "Clean up your own backyard first." Right?

So many paths to these familiar lessons. So many ways to serve the revolution. So many chasms. The potential for bridge building seems endless. Cause for joy or despair? Joy.

Love,
Chris

Reflections on coming out

> My experiments have not been conducted in the closet, but in the open.
>
> Mahatma Gandhi

> Self-disclosure is the one means, perhaps the most direct, by which self-alienation is transformed into self-realization.
>
> Sidney Jourard

Dear Chris,

Thank you for your letter. Your blend of revelation and risking makes for fascinating reading and I find it a gratifying affirmation of our friendship. As you rev up for your next installment, let me offer some thoughts on risk and self-revelation.

I hear there are four essential kinds of risk: the risk one must accept; the risk one can afford to take; the risk one cannot afford to take; and the risk one cannot afford *not* to take.

Far be it from societally-secure-and-supported heterosexual me to tell my gay friends to go public with their sexual identity at work, with family, and beyond. It can be a foolish catch-22 and a bad risk for some lesbians and gays to take. The high cost of remaining invisible might be worth paying.

Nonetheless, when you shared with Carolyn and me, years back, your coming-out letter to your parents, it was a breakthrough moment for you and a vicariously treasured one for us. It was the risk you could not afford *not* to take. You drew your soul forth from its shelter. Your integrity, combined with abiding affection for your parents, stood as a courageous model for us all.

Chris, in your landmark rite-of-transition, you demonstrated that authenticity is the cornerstone of adult existence. To be authentic means to be veritable, trustworthy, not imaginary, false or an imitator. It is our religious summons, from birth on, to be congruent, self-consonant creatures. For when we come to the close of our earthly journey, we will be asked: "How did you complete or fulfill your particular being?" not "How did you conserve or hide yourself?" In the novel *Zorba the Greek*, Zorba and his friend are talking about the friend's character. Zorba comments:

> . . . the same thing's happened to you as happened to the crow. "What happened to the crow, Zorba?" "Well, you see, he used to walk respectably, properly—well, like a crow. But one day he got it into his head to try and strut about like a pigeon. And from that time on the poor fellow couldn't for the life of him recall his own way of walking. He was all mixed up, don't you see? He just hobbled about."

Swiss psychotherapist Paul Tournier said it succinctly: "True guilt is precisely the failure to dare to be oneself."

What makes the leap of authenticity so arduous, and often so anguishing, for gays and lesbians, victims of sexual exclusionism by our heterosexist culture, is that, as someone remarked, "other minorities have everything to gain by demanding their rights; gays and lesbians have everything to lose." There is a cartoon which says: "I only opened up to tell you I'm closed!" In fact, writes our Unitarian Universalist friend Eric Schuman:

> A number of gays and lesbians who have candidated openly and been rejected by numerous congregations throughout our country have gone back into the closet, hidden their sexual identity and been grabbed by congregations looking for a *forthright* candidate!

You know, Chris, one of the distinctive features of our humanity is our capacity to be self-revealing. You and I are the only ones who can disclose our respective interiors, our secrets, our universes. Sisters and brothers can nourish and nudge us, but ultimately each of us vacates our closet(s) in our own fashion and time.

Kenneth Fremont-Smith talks about the relevance and power of the classic gay concept of "coming out" when he pens:

> Coming out is anger: fighting back against bigotry and senseless fear. Coming out is pride: finding dignity and joy in who I am. Coming out is strength: standing tall and taking risks in the world, no longer divided against myself. And coming out is compassion. For if I can celebrate *my* uniqueness, surely I can celebrate the uniqueness of others. If I can name *my* pain and acknowledge its truth, then I can listen to the pain of others. And only then can we join together in common cause. Make no mistake: a single person's coming out shakes the chains of the world. I still got a ways to go. Now that I've found there's more than one closet to come out of, I'm that much more aware of how easy it is to hide. Being in a closet, after all, is safe. The only thing safer is being in a coffin.

"Coming out" is one of the expansive, liberating metaphors of our generation, Chris, and reminds us that we all have closets in which we hover and hide, smothering ourselves amidst the mothballs. I have emerged from a few self-imposed closets of fear and cowardice thus far in my life yet have more to empty in the days ahead. If I'm brave enough.

One final thought. Coming out of our closets is critical but insufficient work. It's the first stage. Then, we gays, straights, and bisexuals alike must let others come in, farther in, still farther into our lives so that authentic, bridging community may begin.

I consider our friendship an effort in the pursuit of authenticity-in-community.

Your friend,
Tom

Love chronicles, part one

Dear Tom,

Ready for the next installment? I thought I'd go back and construct a history from puberty on. Isn't that when life gets interesting anyway? I should say that my own official history is only as good as my memory and sometimes far more selective. I guess we all do our own history, huh?

In 1963, at age 13, I moved with my family to California just before my 9th-grade school year. I was denied a term as student body president of the junior high school I left behind in New Mexico. Everything would change as I arrived in my new home.

I no longer had friends, good feelings about myself, a social milieu that I loved, the urge to dance, laugh, and play. All gone. I no longer found girls and boys fun to be with. I clung to my brothers—my traveling pack of best friends—and our little tract home. I took some comfort in the familiar shrubs we chose to anchor each stucco wall. And I found new favorites in this hot, dry climate—non-bearing mulberry trees that doubled in size every year and wisteria with glorious purple blossoms, above and below.

I felt ugly, unloved, unlovable and caught in a swirl of new faces—a parade of smirking, cliquish classmates who alternately ignored me and then expected too much from me. (I believe I've just penned an operational definition for adolescence.) A girl I befriended in English expected me to make out with her; another girl from up the street talked endlessly with me about her boyfriends and suddenly expected me to cuckold them all; a girl from the volleyball team—bright, sensitive, a little plump, and as awkward as I—yearned for deeper feelings to develop between us.

I seemed incapable of responding and unworthy of this attention and yet, at the same time—with the pride of a young prince who'd been banished from his own homeland and whose charms had evaporated as he left its borders—I also felt everyone unworthy of *my* attentions. Though my pain was concealed, I prayed to make my pain manifest in the lives of those who circled and taunted me.

As people grew frustrated with my unresponsiveness, I grew more obstinate. Prescriptions for behavior and feelings were offered by friends and foes alike. I felt the threat of being partitioned, my energies squandered on a detestable mob. These pressuring peers couldn't understand that my survival actually required me to show no emotional inclinations at all.

I can't remember even being interested in boys during this first year or two of high school. With a few exceptions—one of them a fellow swimmer who had also moved from New Mexico. An errant urge to protect the bloodlines, I suppose. Everyone in California seemed ugly, wicked, sharp-featured, and cruel. A review of my yearbooks fails to confirm these impressions. In retrospect, I seemed to first strip individuals down to protoplasm and then festoon them with goblinesque features.

Where was the passion I had felt earlier in my life? Would I have turned as emotionally introverted back in New Mexico, my lost homeland? Was this personality implosion actually a growing awareness of my attraction to boys? Did I intend to stunt my own growth? When I did manage some semblance of a dating pattern, I harbored tremendous feelings of anxiety and deception—along with all the other feelings that I had learned to associate with interpersonal involvement. All the companions of love.

Whatever social acceptance did grace my life, it seemed a tenuous connection to a shadow world. Even after several years, the prince could find little comfort in this new land. I forged my armor from native materials—shallow friendships, a cynical wit, and a sharp tongue—and from familiar ones as well that had survived my exile—insightfulness, academic skills, an overly competitive spirit, and a strong family pride. The armor worked. It seemed that I might find a new place of distinction in this demiworld.

As hope of a triumphant return to the kingdom faded, I clung to the few Spartan comforts that my new armored existence afforded me. And I began to distrust that part of me that still dreamed—every night—of a life without armor, without guile, and without deception. I had internalized my own banishment. Over my armor, I had donned the mantel of this new oppressive life.

This writing stirs up so many awkward, painful memories. Let me try to articulate the endless questioning I engaged in: Was I cursed to live an armored existence? I was searching for someone—some person who had to embody an entire, lost world—who might remove my armor, presumably as my Self-Oppressor slept. Would I allow someone this honor? Was my dis-enchantment reversible? Had I somehow deserved my fall from grace?

So many questions. They still set off alarms that ricochet through my organs and cells. "I grow weary from so many visions," sighs the misfortune teller. "Enough for now."

Love,
Chris

Bisexuality

> Straddling lives, pulling taut the lines of communication between two very different worlds, finding rare and often claustrophobic pockets of acceptance is what awaits bisexuals who come out.
>
> Michael Ambrosino

Dear Chris,

I used to dismiss bisexuals as persons who were immobilized by indecisiveness, indiscriminately promiscuous, trying to be all things to all people, phonies who were really heterosexual or homosexual and ought to come clean.

Then, especially through the Bisexual Forum that gathers at our church, I met and have grown to respect some individuals who claim that bisexual behavior is, for them, the pinnacle of sexual honesty and fulfillment. One starts to wonder whether we all are or should be bisexual. Maybe it *is* the preference of preferences. As a friend of ours once said, sincerely and with a glow: "My dream is to sit between a man and a woman, fondling both of them at the same time."

I don't seriously question the legitimacy of my own heterosexuality, but I am less smug about my choice than I used to be. My hunch is that we reside on a heterosexual–bisexual–homosexual continuum and, given caring, comfortable conditions, could be more sexually versatile (emotionally and behaviorally) than we ever imagine.

As Adrienne Rich reminds us: "Truth is increasingly complex." It sure is.

Your friend,
Tom

Love chronicles, part two

Dear Tom,

I found your letter about bisexuality interesting on a personal level. There was a period of time when I considered myself a bisexual. I have to remind myself that not all bisexuals are simply homosexuals "in transition" as I was. That's too convenient an explanation and unfairly dismisses a legitimate sexual orientation. Anyway, back to the personal angle . . .

My experience with women is limited. If I encountered a homophobe who was only too willing to explain my sexual orientation as purely a choice, I would ask them, "How long should I have tried to physically love a woman, waiting for my heart to follow? Could you have promised me fulfillment after the first night? The tenth? The hundredth? Could I reasonably have expected sexual satisfaction after a year? After a wedding? After a 25th anniversary? Should I have pledged a lifetime to such a noble experiment?" The experience didn't deliver what it promised and I dropped out. My heart and body could not follow that path.

I think solemnly of how many men have pushed on, bowing to society's pressures, some of them aching for release. Why has enslavement of the individual to the majority always come so naturally to our species? Why do we so seldom make room for variation, much less encourage it? Why are we so afraid—all of us—of differentness?

So many questions. Fewer answers. I mentioned having a crush on boys at earlier ages. That was not a fluke. (It still happens every time I go through the grocery store.) In my twenties, I dated a woman for a year and a half while I harbored a burning desire to ravage a male friend. Any depth of experience I gained from my physical relationship with Laurel was largely stimulated by an unquenchable passion for Jeremy. Occasionally, I still dream of him and in my dreams I improve upon reality. Jeremy finally yields to my advances. Our libidos join and press themselves into a single-celled animal.

I received a baby announcement from Laurel and her husband a few weeks back. I thought of the quantities of seed I had pumped inside her agile and responsive body. Laurel moved on from her "gay" boyfriend—she knew all along, silently—and now has another child. As I felt a twinge of envy for Laurel's good fortune, I thought fondly of the little jokes and rituals we shared a million years and a lifetime ago. And true to my pattern, as I thought of Laurel, I thought of Jeremy—his hard, chiseled body and fathomless mind—and my cock swelled against my jeans and the immediacy of passion, and many of the familiar companions of love, enveloped me.

I didn't need more nights with Laurel. Thank God she moved on and we disrupted each other's lives as little as we did. What I did need was a man who would love me fully. I only succeeded in dabbling with sexual intimacy while learning (or further ingraining) some bad habits. Like self-deception. Like self-denial. Like self-destruction.

As Sondheim says, "I'm still here."

But, Tom, the same cannot be said for many, many young people who self-extinguished as they struggled to connect their inner and outer realities. I am grateful for my continuing experience on this earthly plane. To live *is* to love again.

Love,
Chris

Fidelity

If you are happy, I will give you an apple, if you are
anxious, I will twist your arm, and if you permit me, I
will be glad to hold you close to my heart forever
and do you no harm.

If I am happy, will you give me an apple? If I am
anxious, you may twist my arm. And if you would like
to, I would like you to hold me close to your heart
forever and do me no harm.

This is a bargain, only two can make it. This is a
covenant offered with desperate calm, it being
uncertain that lovers can drive out demons with the
gift of an apple or the twist of an arm.

Tennessee Williams

Dear Chris,

This is a bridging poem for me. It was composed by one of
the 20th Century's finest gay poet–playwrights, and I have em-
ployed it regularly at marriages and services of union. It seems to
strike a responsive chord in our hearts, be we gay or straight.

I definitely believe that our committed partnerships are
"covenants offered with desperate calm," balancing acts that require our boldest array of gifts—ranging from delicious apples to
twisted arms. The twisting process sounds hurtful, but a tweak,
pinch, nudge, or gentle yank make good sense to me as we
friends and lovers risk affection with one another.

But what does fidelity mean? Is it a viable pattern in today's
world or is it rather a highly promoted yet poorly practiced heterosexual relic? What is the role of variety and autonomy in our
love relationships?

Chris, I would covet your responses on the topic of perma-
nence versus fluidity in partnerships. Altman's book, *The
Homosexualization of America,* is the most incisive, germinal volume

I've read on gay life. He constantly stretches my mind, often makes me uneasy. One of his evocative paragraphs reads:

> It is my hunch that the illusion of love is more important for homosexual couples than for heterosexual ones, because without it there is much less reason to persist with the relationship, and this becomes truer as the overt gay world grows and there is less fear of never meeting anyone else. At the same time, while homosexuals may well have more illusions about love, they also have fewer illusions about permanence . . .

I personally hold that freedom and fidelity need not be opponents and that a sexual relationship of worth includes ample spontaneity yet staying power. As gays and straights, our aspiration should be neither casual encounters nor wedlock but full-bodied and full-spirited Eros: relationships of durability, imagination, passion, and playfulness.

I resist the tendency among us all to create liaisons or partnerships of either dependence (the dominance–subjugation pattern) or independence (two self-serving isolates) when we can choose the benefits of interdependence (equality of respect and mutuality of care) in our sexual pairings. I sometimes wonder if I'm an obsolete idealist.

As you share with me your story of emotional and sexual development, I am curious to glean your attitudes about so many aspects of human behavior. Fidelity is just one of them.

Your friend,
Tom

Love chronicles, part three

Dear Tom,

Gather round, listeners. Time for another installment of the love chronicles.

I'm picking this up from the time I moved to San Diego. I quit high school teaching and enrolled in a Master's program in Radio and TV at SDSU. New city. New life. I was ready. "Is this where I'll come out?" The question resounded inside my ascending consciousness. I nearly fell in love with my straight roommate but, through the strength of our longtime friendship, I managed to bypass the drama that I had earlier learned to associate with the phenomenon. Even I had grown weary of this game. We may develop behavior patterns in our lives but we don't always like them.

I worked as a waiter after the first semester and for the first time began to take steps toward my new identity as a gay man. Was I recruited? No. Rescued, maybe. Who knows how long I'd have taken to make the transition on my own. For me, a small town had been a chrysalis without the promise of metamorphosis. And how many women and how many straight men would I have terrorized?

Soon I felt ready for my first sexual relationship with a man (not my first encounter, mind you), a boyish, handsome young man who worked in the kitchen. I allowed myself to lust fully as I stood next to him one day as he studied a recipe in *Bon Apetit*. His fingernails, ears, hair, nose, and eyes—everything about him—fascinated me. I stood close enough to feel his body heat and it warmed me to the core. I suffered in sweet agony for weeks, but a few weeks of anticipation was heaven compared to the patterns of approach and collision I usually engaged in. Although I knew little about his life, I was determined to become his boyfriend. My long dormant passion—my long-hidden desire to explore physical intimacy with a man had left the starting gate. Win, place, or show, I was in the race and not about to turn back.

That was many years ago. I feel as strongly about him as I

did then though countless experiences have tempered our relationship. He still fascinates me. And now, after these many years, I have deep appreciation for his mind and talents. And I have also gained a healthy respect for his foibles, his quirks, and his difficulties in returning my love. Exhilaration and disappointment have both been companions of my love for Rathbun.

Some time later, I dated David. We never lived together but became good companions and compatible sexual partners. I was usually a bit surprised by his appetite for sex but just as often appreciative that he kept things as active as he did. One winter he went to Florida to work with his brother and to visit with his parents. He had some personal concerns and a livelihood in San Diego had seemed elusive. It was hard to see him go. We wrote cards and called each other. In his absence I dated others but I always ended up missing David. I missed the fun and the communication. I missed the honesty and the caring we showed each other. Maybe it was the first time I had been able to develop some positive "companions of love." In his letters, David was beginning to sound like he might not return. I didn't like that at all. Florida was not his future I determined.

I decided to fly to Florida and drive back to California with him. The few days we spent in Florida were great. Visits with his brother's family, hitting the bars, his workplaces, and meeting his friends. We laughed about how I was perceptive enough to immediately ascertain who he'd slept with. And then the long drive home, a journey of many wonders awash in mediocrity: motel rooms, bland food, waitresses who whispered about the two men who bickered as they ordered for each other, long-sweeping Interstates, and more beauty in the South than I'd ever allowed my prejudiced self to imagine. I loved our one steamy afternoon in New Orleans though the city's charm was too gritty for David. We spent two days in San Antonio with his friends from the Western bar he'd hit on the way east.

When we stopped to visit my cousin Janet in Las Cruces, she discovered she had a gay cousin. The tip-off was a modest enough request: we wanted to sleep together on the fold-out couch. She acceded graciously. Then on to Tucson to stay with more of David's friends. In Tucson, I cooled our resumed sexual relationship with an atypically assertive statement: "But I don't want to have sex!" It seemed simple enough but, knowing he'd make me talk about it, it was a brave announcement. I usually avoided talking. David taught me to talk honestly about my feelings and about myself.

Having survived the last 400 miles with a Mexican indigo snake coiled in a pillow case at my feet (David's prize from a fellow herpetologist at the Sonora Desert Museum), we made it back to San Diego. David stayed with me a few weeks while he got a job and a place to live. My camouflage behavior had returned and David sometimes discerned my feelings and spoke for both of us. I seemed reduced to nodding or flaring. "I think both of us are in love with our ex-boyfriends," he declared one day. That would be Rathbun for me, which came as no surprise, I just didn't know it showed. For him, it was Randy, a little traffic stopper with a quiet manner and loins that pleaded for attention. I understood the attraction between them. David's declaration gave us the permission to drift somewhat further apart.

David found work and moved in with a friend who headed up the AIDS Project. The next few months were stormy for the Project, for its director, and for David. Facing adversity head on, David gained a greater acceptance of his own health conditions. As autumn approached, David began dating a preppy blond number and wove sex back into the healing fabric of his life. The intensity of it all may also have contributed to the rapid decline of his new relationship even as a month earlier the intensity had fueled it. Certain energies, uncertain times.

By now, David and I had established an abiding friendship. And in the late fall of 1985, we let our friendship flower into romance one last time—we'd be boyfriends through the holidays, we decided. And so we were—from Thanksgiving through my birthday and all the way through Christmas and New Year's. The ending date having been set perhaps allowed me to relax just enough that I enjoyed David as much as I ever had. And we had a strong friendship for added depth. It was a wonderful time.

A few days after the first of the year, David took up with someone new. I was annoyed and relieved in equal measures. David and Anthony are together today, years later and I treasure my friendship with them both.

Tom, I have this image of my announcing the end of story time, closing a big, leather-bound book, and tucking you in for a safe and dreamful sleep. "Yes, the prince is safe for now. We'll continue our story tomorrow, Thomas. Now it's time for *all* princes to get some sleep."

Good night,
Chris

None of my business

Dear Chris,

This is a none-of-my-business letter, born of bias and affection.

I recognize that most sexual connections, gay and straight alike, reside somewhere on a continuum between the promiscuous and the permanent. Yet I fear that our American society has grown all too accustomed, almost enamored, of transiency in relationships and what Beverley Hotchner calls "a throwaway lifestyle" where recreational, faceless sex becomes common and acceptable.

My own record is checkered. I failed at my first marriage, yet am currently grounded, happily so, in a committed partnership which, barring a catastrophe, will take me to the grave.

As I learn about a few of your deeper love ties, Chris, I can't help but wonder: Is permanent commitment in the cards for you? Is marriage, however interpreted or solemnized, a reality with meaning for you?

As long as I'm getting personal (which is what these letters are all about—getting personal without being intrusive or unduly private), let me reiterate how profoundly moved I was by your brave and anguished disclosure, before 300 of us during a gay-lesbian worship service in Palm Springs, that not having children was one of the great sadnesses in your life. It brought tears to my eyes, because I have seen you with children, and know that you would make a wonderful father.

I hope that during our time together—running, singing, talking, and listening—we find time to talk about fatherhood.

Your friend,
Tom

Love chronicles, part four

Dear Tom,

It's been a while since my last pot-boiler but I'm sure I can bring you right back to the story line. No groaning, now!

I had just concluded (amicably and intentionally) my relationship with David. We were both itching for new romantic adventures. David had just met Anthony and, at about the same time (although deliberately *after* David started dating Anthony), I also started seeing someone new.

It was a busy time for me. Within a few weeks I would mount a major convention for gay men and lesbians from around the country and then I was scheduled to fly to Swaziland, Africa, having been chosen as the first professor in a university-sponsored program on development communications. Somewhere in those few frantic weeks—three at the most—Grant and I got entangled but good!

Jeez, how I latched on. He was bright, witty, aggressive, handsome, young, athletic, talented, and . . . he liked me a whole bunch. "Beyond glandular" I reported to my friend David. We were nearly as nonplused by each other's romances as we were by our own. David still holds a letter that could nominate me as one of the great love puppies of all time.

I cried most of the way to the airport to catch my flight to Africa. Grant was torn between comforting me and holding the steering wheel. Then, when the flight was delayed and a new travel connection was established, we rejoiced in our extra half-day together. We hurried back to his apartment and spent the afternoon in bed digging wildly into the caverns of love.

Africa was a bust. I had never felt so challenged—and so ambushed—in a professional situation. My homesickness and my yearning to be in Grant's embrace were indistinguishable in my aching heart and mind. Our first day together when I returned to San Diego was again spent in bed. Despite my lack of sleep and general travel weariness, I mounted Grant with more purpose and passion than I had ever experienced in my life. We both felt a visceral connection that terrified and thrilled us.

Whereas our limbs and hearts became interwoven with full intention and design, our lives and careers would prove not to mesh with much ease. Shortly after my return, Grant had lined up a job in San Francisco. He'd been job searching for some time. "Come with me, Chris. There's nothing for you here." And the damage phase began.

Grant imagined that together we would become each other's everything. By deduction, our old lives were nothing. And San Diego represented my old life. He overlooked my involvements with church, friends, clubs, teams, and family.

And then there was my long established infatuation with Rathbun, who was now showing up at the house doing little fix-it projects—a couple of cement urns, an iron railing, an old banister for the front porch, a leaded glass window that would adorn the utility room, a window box in the kitchen for herbs. He was irrepressible and ubiquitous. He became Grant's best friend. His constant presence was explained as only wanting to do some nice things for his friend Chris before my "new life" took me away to San Francisco.

With my covert and subconscious encouragement, things got real crazy, real fast. While Grant yanked on my aching body and spirit to go north, Rathbun constructed—with hammer, saw, paint brush, a pile of discards, and his own miraculous hands—an irresistible offering of love. Grant and Rath soon became rival siblings, scrambling to please their parent. My heart was inexorably being won by Rathbun and all of his "temple" building. I would let things escalate for another month before I found the words to speak my heart's decision but that month was anything but a holding pattern. The rivalry intensified, Rathbun worked at the house more and more, Grant became increasingly confrontational with me, and visiting friends looked on with disbelief and horror. As for me, I got constipated.

Rath's addiction to me and (as I began to realize through the fog of craziness) to drugs grew to enormous proportions in the heady ferment of our interpersonal hothouse. Grant, experiencing great loss, disbelief, and imminent life transitions, spilled over with caustic recriminations. I became the benevolent and aloof dictator. I seemed to hold all the cards and I dealt an unyielding and painful hand for everyone at the table. We may all still be recovering from that card game.

In my memory, the next few months spin by in fast-forward mode—living with Rathbun; finishing the house, selling the house, living with his parents, paying off dealers . . . And then, picking him up at the jail one night, I announced, "Enough."

That single word was the turning point but our long slow recovery would never be that simple or that concise. My constant fear was thinking that I had caused the craziness. I was absolutely unable to sort out the boundaries of my own responsibility, for myself or for other people. While Rath was undergoing treatment for drug addiction at the McDonald Center, I felt that our relationship was being trivialized though I seemed too confused to mount any lucid rebuttal. Anger and confusion were my constant companions.

When I visited Rath at the halfway house, I was petrified to hear from his counselor that my continuing to care about Rath would actually contribute to his destruction. With all the diplomacy and reasonableness my shattered psyche could muster, I tried to explain and define a new relationship for us, but Rathbun felt betrayed and oscillated wildly between hating me and loving me. As Rathbun completed his stay at the ranch and returned to town, he moved back in with an ex-lover and I was frozen with rage.

Would I ever find equilibrium in this torment?

More to follow,
Chris

Loving the distance

But, once the realization is accepted that even between the closest human beings infinite distances continue to exist, a wonderful living side by side can grow up, if we succeed in loving the distance between us which makes it possible for each to see the other whole and against a wide sky!

Rainer Maria Rilke

We can be Other without being Enemy. We can also be friends.

John Nierenberg

Dear Chris,

Pluralism reigns supreme within the gay male world. Gays and lesbians also display marked distinctions, on matters ranging from lifestyles to pornography to feminism. It is no surprise, then, that gay and straight cultures exhibit differences as well.

Indeed, as a modern commentator noted, the bedroom may be one place where we straights and gays don't differ all that much. It's outside the bedroom that lifestyle eccentricities are more noticeable.

I know, Chris, that there are elements in the gay world that are foreign, occasionally bothersome, to me. You have to live in a predominantly straight society; you know how to make the necessary adjustments to survive. I am far less versed in the customs, language, and literature of the gay scene. Despite growing familiarity, I remain a relative neophyte.

We whites like to talk about being color–blind, when this is but a subtle way to perpetuate racism. Skin color does, in fact, matter in our society and always will as long as gross injustices result from it. Similarly, progressive straights are quick to gloss over glaring differences that exist between gays and straights, thereby perpetuating current phobias and biases. We must mature to the stage where being gay and being straight are equally valid and valued life-choices rather than promoting a social system that encourages gays to imitate straights.

Chris, by participating in recent years, for example, in Gay Pridefest events I have gained greater exposure to and understanding of the gay culture. But even if I share in such activities until the close of my life, I will always feel somewhat alien to your chosen milieu. Don Kilhefner writes that the dilemma facing gay men is "our assimilation into the mainstream versus our enspiritment as a people. . . . There is a reality to being Gay that is radically *different* from being Straight. . . . It is real. We can feel it in our hearts and in our guts."

Such differentness presents neither an insurmountable obstacle nor an undesirable one. All I'm saying, Chris, is that in our quest to be better friends, the fruitful path lies not in blurring our dissimilarities, or in tolerating them, but in genuinely recognizing them, learning from them, occasionally celebrating them.

You and I will always be different in so many ways: some because of background, others because of personality, still others because of our sexual orientation. Just know that I appreciate the fact that we are two independent individuals who refuse to run or cling. In being your friend I am learning how to befriend someone of my own gender, male like myself, as well as someone quite different from me—a gay man. Both present imposing yet nourishing tasks.

So, our letters symbolize the sharing of minds and souls from a distance—a distance that gives us perspective and honors our private sensibilities, a distance that grants us renewed interest in and gratitude for the Other, a distance that encourages us to grow close without minimizing our gulf.

We both acknowledge that "loving the distance between us" is the mission of expansive friendship.

Your friend,
Tom

Love chronicles, part five

Dear Tom,

In my ongoing tale, I was last seen at the bottom of a deep well. Just one direction to go, right? I'm skipping over a few years, not because they were uneventful but because what these years of recovery and healing gave me can best be appreciated by looking at the relationship they prepared me for.

Dan didn't arrive all at once. I'd met him when he was dating a friend of mine several years earlier and liked him immediately. Something solid. Something gentle. Something good-looking, too. Now, that I've been dating him for several months, I think: "This man may be my match."

We talk—even though it's difficult sometimes. We both have past loves we wrestle with. We have sex that keeps getting better though exploration is careful. Still, I seem to suffer an emotional tentativeness. And yet I anxiously await surrender. More to be revealed.

Recently, Dan and I had a nice breakfast that he prepared at his place. We had spent the night before at my house and I had gone off to run with Front Runners, my gay running group that meets at the park every Saturday (with or more often without me). As I walked into Dan's downtown loft, I saw ingredients piled in the blender, his hand poised on the power switch. "Smoothie?" he asked.

Breakfast was nourishing, gratifying, and lovingly presented. Scrambled eggs, peanut butter on English muffins, and some strong coffee with cream. Best of all, a beautiful, gentle breakfast partner. It doesn't get any better than this, I thought to myself.

We relaxed and talked the rest of the morning—about our lives, about our struggle as artists to mix discipline with our longing for expression and the self-permission to give that expression its fullest dimensions.

As we sat on the couch, I looked at his wide, Nordic face and pretty blue eyes and said, "You are so good looking!"

"I don't think so, " he responded, a little uneasy. I knew what he meant. But as a visual artist, it must be different for him. His aesthetic may not be yielding enough to see his own beauty. But he sees mine. And I see his. And as we begin to believe in each other, we also believe in ourselves.

And I wonder, will I let him into my life? I've teased myself with the notion and as I take little tastes of that reality, I've wanted more. I'm aware of a deep stirring. I'm filled with incipient longing for a partnership with this man.

I pause at the edge of a mountain pond. It promises refreshment, depth, and so many pleasures. I dance, uncertain and barefoot, on his circling lips.

All for now,
Chris

Straight but not narrow

Dear Chris,

As I reflect back upon my own rather stable yet boring sexual history, I am struck by its slow yet relentless heterosexual development. While I loved jousting and wrestling physically with my boyhood chums, I never once doubted or questioned, and, therefore, never really chose my heterosexuality. I simply evolved an awakened attraction towards and arousal alongside women.

Growing up I was adept at choosing safe, non–physical, romantic gambits in relating to girls rather than employing the more aggressive, bodily tactics of some peers. I was sexually naive, somewhat repressed, until my late teen years, when my "straight" path curved and squiggled some. I clumsily yet inexorably moved over a period of years toward sexual intimacy with the woman whom I would eventually marry. I remember being caught off guard, a bit ashamed, and pleasurably surprised, by my first orgasm during heavy petting.

But unlike my gay brothers, I never was impelled to ask myself, "Am I straight or am I gay?" Once my sexual awakening took place, the only issues that ever emerged have been ones of adequacy and enjoyment. I have quivered occasionally with doubts, yet my bedrock sexual identity has remained solid, unshaken.

The word "straight," I am told, comes from the root meaning "stretched." I must admit that during my sexual journey from uptightness through an insecure, wandering period in young adulthood, until now being happily ensconced in a straightforward, straightlaced partnership with my wife, I have seldom been stretched or challenged as a sexual being. It seems to me, Chris, that gay men are the ones who have been stretched, often painfully so. My biological, romantic inclinations have invariably been assisted and sanctioned by the social mores of a heterosexist culture. So, it remains my moral imperative as a heterosexual person in places of privilege and power in our society to be a pliant, supple straight man—firm but not rigid, a straight man who dares to be frank but not unbending—in short, a straight man without being a narrow one.

   As I re-read this simple and truthful epistle, Chris, I'm afraid my sexual odyssey doesn't sound very interesting, certainly not as eventful as yours, noticeably void of the sudden shifts and stirring juices that have filled the entries in your "love chronicles." But how could it be otherwise? Our sexual orientations are different, our personalities are different, our ways of self-disclosure are different. *Vive la différence!*

Your friend,
Tom

Into the Woods . . . and Back

> Whatever you have to say, leave the roots on, let them dangle, and the dirt, just to make clear where they come from . . .
>
> Charles Olson

Dear Chris,

Here's a letter direct from my cabin in the woods to your house in the city.

As you know, I am presently nestled amidst the Temeculan forest at the Dorland Mountain Arts Colony, exploring the expanses of nature and fathoming the secrets of my soul. For five dollars a day, I am dwelling in an unheated shack, utterly alone, for the month of February. Calls to my wife and occasional notes to friends like you comprise the extent of my civilization. The bulk of my life here in the woods is unstructured, wild, without human contact. An unusual yet blessed immersion for me.

In nearly five decades of existence this is the lengthiest, spartan excursion I've ever endured. Upon waking early in the morning, each day is entirely mine to shape from interior yearnings not external obligations. I may never enjoy such a precious, unfettered expanse of solitude again, so I am surrendering myself to its mysteries.

Chris, I am fitfully learning that the soulful life has primarily to do with tilling the humus rather than sailing the sky. My tendency, as a buoyant personality, is to fly away to the light whenever darkness appears—resisting opportunities to mulch my moist soil. Being a child of enlightenment and bathed in a culture of rationalism and stoicism makes purposeful descent into the shadowy recesses of one's psyche a rare adventure. I invariably ignore the truth that I, a full-blooded descendant of Adam, am a child of slimy mud. Consequently, it is with ample trepidation I have undertaken to cultivate my inner soil and reconnect with any and all dangling, dirt-laden roots.

Halfway into this pilgrimage in the dank woods, I can report to you, Chris, that I have been grappling daily and nightly with angst, anger, and anguish—distinct yet related soulful demons of the netherworld. I confess that my life-long inclinations have invariably been to eradicate fear, to flush rage, and to smother grief, but wandering off by myself in the woods for weeks has opened me up to welcoming these foreigners into the household of my being.

Angst—a word which sounds as frightful and tenacious as the existential anxiety to which it refers. Angst, angst, angst. Here at Dorland there are unnerving animal sounds at night and untamed beasties roaming about in my daytime dreamworld. With neither deities nor earthlings rushing in to rescue me, I am left alone to face the onslaught of angst as baldly and bravely as I can. I am surviving, my friend.

Anger. Sauntering through the sagebrush I discover myself emitting weird growls, perhaps acknowledging, then releasing, in this solitary environs, the private tiger prowling within my soul. Chris, as you have already grown to know, my maturity level in expressing robust anger would place me in an emotional grade school. I yearn to be resolutely angry rather than sloshing about in the swamps of passive-aggression. Whether in marriage or parenting, work or friendships, my goal remains to care enough to give people a more unabridged version of myself—including clumsy, combustible sentiments like anger.

Anguish. Oddly enough, I find myself crying frequently at Dorland. Tears of sadness but tears of gratitude, confusion, and delight as well. Following in the footsteps of my woodsman-friend Doug von Koss, I feel sufficiently unjudged and free in the wilderness to allow tears to wet my cheeks, staying there, instead of being compulsively wiped off. The tears just come now, linger awhile, then cascade to the ground.

So, these three—angst, anger, and anguish—are among the strange yet welcome companions during my soul-journey amidst our majestic, gnarled Southern Californian woods. I'll have more stories and ample silence to share when I see you in early March.

Your friend,
Tom

Too close for comfort?

Dear Tom,

During February, I often thought of you in your wooded retreat at Dorland. Sometimes I have had glimpses into your very being; it almost seems too close for comfort. Like barging in on you in your spiritual bathroom. We all have one. It's that place where we alternate between feeling alone (because we've been taught to lock the door?) and feeling connected to all things (because we do fundamental things in there).

Am I too flippant to continue this line of thought? The "parentheses index" suggests that I'm not quite focusing. All this commentary. It so often gets in my way. Like I was a cynical, defensive teenager again. Like a lot of bad habits, cynicism may have been my survival at one point but it also robs me of the opportunity to move beyond the easy reaction.

I took some notes during your talk on the Sunday you returned to the pulpit. You spoke as if you were still a bit dazed— spinning with metaphors and rich imagery. The mystic, bearded and hallucinating, returning from the mountain top—almost like you wanted to keep us at arm's length and to keep your primal forest experience lodged in your heart and tissues. We were no more eager to break the spell than you so it was a remarkable situation—an exercise in delightful complicity. I said during our Tuesday run that your talk and your reporting to our smaller men's group was like the honeybee's dance. We felt compelled to watch whether or not we planned on harvesting the same field of flowers. Whether or not we might one day retreat to the woods for our own month of solitude.

There were two things you shared that Sunday morning I'd like to comment on. First, you borrowed from the writings of feminist women authors: Alice Walker, Toni Morrison, and others. By your own admission, you didn't want to overload the experience with male-identified energies. Why not? I respect your instinct, but I can't help being curious about whatever fears or dangers are implicit in your choice. Is there a male image deep inside that you turn away from? So that's one. Let's talk about it.

Second, the quote you shared that has been attributed to Jesus by the Gnostics: "Bring forth what is within you and what is within you will save you. If you do not bring forth what is within you, it will destroy you." Isn't that it, then? Let's all stop talking, go home, and just ponder that message. Let's look inside for what is within each of us. A treasure hunt that only requires a team of one. "You gotta walk that lonesome valley. You gotta walk it by yourself."

There's always the communal campfire to balance the solitude of those journeys for single travelers. Hey, is that what our men's group is, a campfire which we gather around, our backs to the cold and dark? You know, Tom, I don't think I've ever had as clear an understanding as you of what our men's group was about, aside from the obvious support and discussion opportunities. But I'm committed to the enterprise. Anyway, I digress . . . appropriately, but I digress.

Thanks for sharing with us your experience in the woods, Tom. I want to know how you plan to revisit this new spiritual real estate that you have acquired. I know it won't sit unworked.

It gives a whole new meaning to the expression, "Meanwhile, back at the ranch . . . "

Love,
Chris

*Dan created this image of his healing place and sent it out
to friends and family shortly after having brain surgery.*

A Time for Healing

I wish that I had written more letters to Tom during the first year of my relationship with Dan. It was a wonderful time of growth—individually and for our partnership. Maybe that's why I seemed to have less time for writing letters! It was also a time of renewed creative endeavor—Dan with his painting and me with singing and songwriting.

At the end of our first year, Dan was diagnosed with a brain tumor and within hours was on the operating table in what I knew was truly a life or death situation. Dan wasn't able to focus his mental powers so he didn't feel much anxiety, but I wasn't so lucky. My consciousness was filled with a quiet terror. I feared losing him.

However, the operation which "de-bulked" the orange-sized tumor was a success and he began a miraculous recovery. Two months later we took a trip to Vancouver, British Columbia to attend the Gay Games, an Olympics-styled sports festival for gay men and lesbians from around the world. I know the only reason I won my butterfly medal was that I could see his pretty, bandana-wrapped head at the far end of the pool.

Dan grew up in northern Idaho and went to school in Oregon, but this was my first trip to the Northwest. Both of us were eager to return for a longer trip so he could *really* show me around. We planned a month-long car trip in the fall that would include visits with his parents, grandparents, and *great*-grandmother. We also planned to visit his brother, sisters, and their families. Somewhere in there we would manage to do a fair amount of sight-seeing and enjoy each other's company.

During our pilgrimage, I kept a travel diary and wrote letters to Tom. I wanted to chronicle what I knew would be an important trip as Dan continued his recovery from brain surgery and we opened ourselves to new levels of adventure and intimacy.

Northwest passage

Dear Tom,

    This is the first time that I've sat down to write to you since Dan and I began our trip—our "Northwest Passage," as we call it. About an hour north of San Diego, we stopped in for a short but invigorating visit with Mom and Dad—our loving well wishers. We even scored an apple pie to take with us on the first leg of our journey. How many times have I driven away from those two, watching them in my rear-view mirror and wondering just how deep a parent's love for children must be?

    We pushed on to my friend Kim's in West Hollywood. Dan turned in early and Kim and I, anxious to catch up on all the things good friends fuss over, headed out for dinner. True to the oscillating nature of most friendships, Kim and I travel the continuum between near symbiosis and, at the other end, being almost careless in the attention we give our friendship. On this night we floated somewhere between these two poles. I had hoped to communicate more. I wanted Kim to understand just how important this trip was to me. We delighted in perusing the menu, ordering, and then gobbling some really tasty Chinese food and I was reminded that the immediacy of experience—especially when it includes food and drink—often distracts us from attending to our other needs.

    Kim tangled stares with several of the good-looking men who had gathered in this dinner house on Melrose Ave. There's joy in just watching male animals interact. Kim celebrated each returned smile and, as we walked back to the car, we replayed the interactions once or twice more. Dan and I made a bed on Kim's living room floor and I remember thinking how nice it was to get past the stares and smiles and flexing with other men—how nice it was to just lie down next to one special man. And then I wondered: "Had I displayed some of this 'relationship smugness' during my evening with Kim?" I hoped not.

    The next morning, Kim headed off to work and Dan and I took a leisurely approach to continuing our trip. We glided along

Sunset to the freeway, passing all those beautiful homes and cars. We really felt like we had done enough of the L.A. thing. Then we headed north on the freeway and over the Tehachipis. As we came down that winding drop into the Central Valley, Dan was sleeping and I made a last minute decision to drive up Interstate 5 on the west side of the valley, knowing I'd have to add some miles at the end of our day to get over to Merced. I just couldn't face Highway 99—all the trucks, the billboards, and the on ramps with slow-moving cars. Interstate 5 was peaceful, smooth, uncrowded, and beautiful. Especially toward the middle of the state when it climbs up a 100 or so feet and you can look across the jillions of acres being farmed, ranched, tilled, watered, harvested . . . worked.

So much of the Valley is always in transition, always producing, always intriguing. My love for the actual real estate, the dirt of the Valley, reminds me that I didn't leave because of the ruralness. Leaving my teaching position had been primarily a psychological move that I played out geographically. I had not been willing—or able—to come out as a gay man in that small Valley town. Now, with each passing mile of our "Northwest Passage," my soul welcomed the openness once again.

As we rolled into Merced, I prepared myself for a constant stream of *deja-vu* experiences.

More later.

Love,
Chris

Oh, Great Spirit!

Dear Tom,

On the second day of our stay in Merced, Dan and I took the two-hour drive to Yosemite National Park. Dan had expressed interest in seeing Yosemite when we first started planning our trip. Arriving in the Park, we found very little water in the streams—nothing visible coming down Yosemite Falls and just a trickle at Bridalveil. We took the loop around the valley floor, stopping several times. Suddenly aware of the impact that all this natural splendor was having on Dan, I followed him out into a meadow. He spoke a prayer to the Great Spirit. I joined him in his moment of reverence, his total surrender to life and beauty. He opened his arms expansively as he spoke, reciting the prayer of Yellow Lark:

> Oh Great Spirit, God-Life
> Whose voice we hear in the wind and
> Whose breath gives life to all the world.
> Hear us! We come to you, two of your many
> children.
> We are small and weak
> We need your strength and wisdom . . .

Dan then added his own words, expressing gratitude for such a beautiful world, for life, and for our partnership. I was held in an embrace of words and wonders as complete as I've ever known. As the sky grew cloudy, we cocked our heads to watch a thrilling ballet of white and blue forms overhead. I opened up to the marvel of sky and stone as if it were my first visit, too.

We returned to the car to drive on to the Awahnee Hotel—a 1927 wood-and-stone hotel with capacious rooms and fireplaces. Dan's love of beauty is not confined to natural wonders. You should have seen his smile of childlike amusement when he posed full height inside one of the large fireplaces. We strolled through the grounds and then, returning to the parking lot, I took the opportunity (have I missed one yet?) to admire our new car. That bright red Jetta really gleams in the greenery of forest and ferns.

Towering walls of granite, threads of water plunging thousands of feet, one architect's inspiration made manifest in a resort hotel, and this little contraption of glass and steel, slapped over with red paint. We love them all!

We headed up to Glacier Point, a rocky outlook several thousand feet vertically situated over the valley floor. We stopped at the Washburn lookout where we could gaze at the upper Merced River Canyon, taking in a side view of Half Dome and other high-country landmarks. A geological sign tried patiently to convey the natural history of the scene. Understanding that scientists had stretched their minds and language to interpret this wondrous scene added to the grandness but, like a passage of literature that momentarily delights and then is soon forgotten, the wonder before me pierced my soul and filled me with spirit, but circumnavigated my faculty for understanding. With some distance and fewer natural distractions, I might be able to follow the geological unfolding and the story might stick. But in the presence of such awesome reality, the story seemed a vanishing echo.

God bless the scientists who keep track of all this stuff! I can't help but wonder if their sense of awe is in some way diminished because they must harness their mental capacity to understand and explain. I guess the great naturalists are led by their spirit, and that their spirit is undampened by their aptitude for analysis. Those skills remain secondary, however sharp and nimble. They blend the energies of their lives with true artistry.

We are artists, one and all. Dan and I stand here, breathing beauty into our hearts and minds to be expressed at some later time in a new painting or a new song. We are all placed on Earth to pursue our artistry. Today is a powerful reminder.

More later,
Chris

The chance to say "thank you"

Dear Tom,

This has been such an amazing day. I know I'm still playing catch up with this journal—we were just in Yosemite, right?—but I must leap ahead and report a fresher story.

We're in the Portland area where Dan taught middle school for five years before moving to San Diego. Even though he's been gone eight years, these people love him and welcome him as a returning brother and son. While he taught at this school, Dan had organized his classes into an army of mural painters. The halls of Renne Middle School still show their good work and the murals are clearly a source of pride for the students today.

What was it Dan's friend Sharon said at the impromptu assembly they organized on his behalf: "So often we're given presents by people and we don't know who they are. Today, we have the chance to say thank you." And they did. A standing ovation as he walked down the aisle of the filled auditorium.

Dan didn't know Sharon had planned the assembly but his instincts must have told him to dress up and he now moved toward the stage confidently, his Panama hat over a light orange bandana. Nice touch that he could tip his hat when he thanked the students and teachers for their outpouring.

"I appreciate your appreciation," he said at the outset. He provided the kids with a little history on the murals, emphasizing how all the students had done the actual painting. He talked about the murals he had created with elementary students in the San Diego area over the past few years. He talked about his brain surgery in May and his remarkable recovery since that time. He told the students that he was now concentrating on his own painting—realistic landscapes. Then he gestured toward the back of the room with an easy naturalness, and introduced his partner Chris who was taking this great trip with him through the Northwest. Having dried my tears and settled down by this time, I got a chuckle out of all the heads pivoting to see this "partner Chris." I looked at Dan, solid and smiling, seemingly unaware of my being doused with curious stares. Soon Dan had their full attention again as he wrapped up his little talk and received another rousing ovation. Sharon then sent the kids back to their fifth-period classes.

Lots of teachers came up to chat with Dan, to hug Dan, to shake the hand of Dan, and to tell him how good it was to see him. As I moved to the front of the hall to join him, Dan introduced me all around. One woman, a PE teacher, took my hand and said, "Thank you for bringing him back. Thank you." Then I was filled with a remarkable sensation—I felt important. And, at the same time, very generous.

That scene at Renne Middle School was nearly too much for words. I was so moved. Dan was so strong, so confident, so warm. I nearly burst with pride, tears, and love all at once. Did Dan's buddy Carol turn to see my chin quivering? Did she study my reaction to determine what secrets about Dan's health we might be hiding? These people care so much about Dan.

I think about Dan's support team in San Diego and I wonder if one of the reasons for this trip is trying to decide where our support might be stronger.

More later,
Chris

In a flurry

Dear Tom,

I called to retrieve my messages from home in San Diego. My sister-in-law Jeni says that Dad has had a heart attack and is having a very difficult time. He's stable but it's very serious and they've had a hard time finding me.

A flurry of calls later, I realized that Dad's condition is still serious. Dan and I talked about what we should do. I knew that I wanted to go home. I suggested that I could fly, leaving the Jetta with Dan so he could push on and visit with his family in Seattle, Spokane, and northern Idaho. We talked it through. Carol looked on, listened and encouraged me to do what was right for me, to take care of myself.

Dan and I have decided to drive back together. We just faced his health emergency together and couldn't imagine facing this new crisis apart. On this night before we begin our return, I am filled with anxiety and, once again, the fear of losing someone I love.

We're coming home.

Love,
Chris

Across ages and miles

Dear Chris,

When you and Dan drove north to visit friends, relatives, and the exquisite countryside (familiar to him yet fresh to you), it was more than merely a month-long jaunt. It had the trappings of a pilgrimage: to bring rest to your fatigued spirit, healing to Dan's ailing body, and renewal to your beleaguered partnership.

I envisioned you leisurely winding your way up our gorgeous Pacific coastline, soaking in the ocean breeze, sauntering among the majestic redwoods, connecting with buddies, feeding your ever-deepening love . . . away from the pressures and regimen of home life on Kansas Street. A month is none too long, my friend, to restore your souls and strengthen your partnership. So, stay away as long as you both need. We can all wait until you are good and ready to return.

After ten or so days on the road, you reached Portland, only to hear the shocking news that your Dad had experienced cardiac arrest and was hospitalized in serious condition in San Diego County. You and Dan rushed back, and along with your brothers and their partners, kept vigil by his side.

As your father launched his slow recovery, you and Dan wisely started back on your sojourn, where I know your spirit must be burdened by the respective illnesses of the two most special men in your life: Dan and your father Frank. I felt honored, Chris, when you asked me to watch over your father, as his minister-friend, while you were away. I will, I will.

I went yesterday to visit your Dad at Scripps Memorial Hospital. Your dear, devoted mother, Doris, ever-smiling, was fast by his side. Upon my arrival, Frank met me with his irrepressible enthusiasm. I have been visiting shut-ins and hospitalized patients for the full twenty-six years of my ministry, but I have rarely seen a heart patient spring with such energy.

But Frank is Frank, and as you well know (since you display some of his same lust for life and genuine exuberance), there are few souls as spirited as your Dad. His voice choked with emotion as he told about the immediate care he received when he slumped unconscious while playing paddle tennis. "They saved my life, they saved my life," he cried.

I probably overstayed my visit, but we couldn't stop gabbing—Doris, Frank, and I. We talked some about their new home, church life, music, and Frank's recent paintings—delightfully rich landscapes.

Most of all, wouldn't you know it, we talked about what we share in common: *you*. He mentioned your specialness as a person, as his son, and tears streamed down my face as I seconded his powerful emotion. Then all three of us proceeded to recount the particular ways in which you are loved and affirmed, special to us as son *and* friend.

As you and Dan re-enter the rain-filled haunts of our Northwest, we shower you with a fountain of affectionate tears from hospital room, No. 309.

Your friend,
Tom

Happy Birthday, Dan

Dear Tom,

What a great day this has been. It's Dan's birthday and we took a trip around the shore of Lake Pend Oreille here in northern Idaho. I wanted to share with you something I wrote in my journal today as we explored this land that nurtured Dan during his childhood and young adulthood. Now it embraces me as well.

Happy Birthday, Dan. You have given me so much on this day. Guiding me on this pilgrimage to the Northwest and taking this day trip around this magical lake. It will nearly embarrass me to give you the simple book and card I bought on the sly today as we kicked around your native Sandpoint. Now we sit on a rocky beach across Lake Pend Oreille from the town. Me, finally scribbling in this journal again and you, putting on a sweater and a stocking cap. The temperature is in the 50s, I would guess. It is overcast but the sky ranges from a glaring white overhead to a heavy gray in the east.

Just stopped at a geological sign that reminded us of this lake's glacial origins. Ice sheets once as high as the mountain tops. Every fact of creation is so amazing! And is that what distinguishes us from the rest of the animal kingdom? A dropping jaw? No, it's the opposing thumb, isn't it? I forget everything in the presence of such majesty. And my mouth hangs open with awe each time I look up from this notebook and gaze upon the water, stretching across to hillsides covered with deep green fir and pine and golden tamarack. The lake shore is almost playful as peninsulas, islands, and the far hills weave rhythmic, echoing lines before me. A marauding shoreline. Every now and then, a wisp of smoke, motionless in this cool, heavy air, indicates the presence of other admirers amid the trees.

Do the residents lose the sense of magic and take all this beauty for granted? I wonder, when do we lose our sense of awe in the presence of such wonder? Maybe it's when we spin our human cocoons of sickening air, artificial materials, and garish colors. Are we the animal that alienates itself from its own origins? Are we evolution's point of departure? If so, we are also capable of being evolution's point of many returns. And each return can be as bracing as a chest–full of glacial air.

And now, the car beckons and my mind and stomach yearn for dinner with Dan's parents, Don and Ruby, in their beautiful hillside dwelling. Life is poised between departure and return. It's where we all live. They are the two directions we alternately take. Like breathing.

The sun peeks through, spilling its light on the water and skipping across waves and rocks to visit me ever so briefly. A sparkling moment of love and fulfillment and endless wonder.

I turn to see Dan, my sweet partner. And I return to the car to join our lives once more.

All for now.

Love,
Chris

Oncology clinic

Dear Tom,

Yes, we're back in San Diego and getting back into our schedules. We seem to be experiencing some small measure of discord in this time of adjustment. Back from the road trip and back to the healing routine.

As we were driving to the oncology clinic to get some blood work for Dan, we each launched a few topics and then kind of picked away at them with half-hearted responses. Then Dan said, "Well, it will be good to see how this . . ."

"Tumor?" I almost said aloud as my thoughts leaped out of their malaise. "Is he bringing it up? Thank you, Dan!" And I reached for his hand as he continued.

" . . . big, old . . ."

Was he saying it *was* big? *Is* big? What *does* he think about it?

" . . . building up here is coming along."

Then I realized he was wondering about the monstrous new building project on Washington Street. I was simultaneously relieved and frustrated that I had misinterpreted his musings.

I tickled that little wart on his palm, he withdrew his hand to hit the blinker, and I too pulled away, splaying my fingers nervously across my thigh.

Tension flows in my life and body. Like a new humor.

All for now.

Love,
Chris

Desert storm

Dear Tom,

I'm stretched out beside a motel pool in Palm Springs. My cheeks will get more color from this wind than from the sun. Yet I stubbornly demand the warmth of a recalcitrant sun.

We bought some groceries last night, trying to set up house in this little motel room. Dan hasn't felt up to going out. I'm surprised we even made the trip to the desert. He had a surge of energy yesterday afternoon so we took the leap. Once again, we answered the call of the open road. Our first escape since our Northwest passage. I think I would have preferred staying home—but that's all the more reason for getting away.

I don't stop at home. A business call, a file folder file on the table—anything can trigger another work session. Suddenly, there I am—sequestered in my office with computer and laser printer, only taking breaks to read to Dan, fix tea, cook a meal, run some errands, or clean up the kitchen. It's a routine with a thousand variations so I never see it for what it is . . . staying occupied. Staying busy. Suspending disbelief. Sustaining life. Aren't those all legitimate? They are my salvation.

I truly think staying occupied is a strength. And I think it fits my new reality and my new commitments—honesty, emotions, growth, expansion. All those things take tending. They take work. New activities. New things to stay busy with . . .

Who am I arguing with? Who am I trying to convince?

A few weeks back, I brought up the subject of wills—that we needed to make them. Dan's illness had made bringing the subject up a bit awkward. We agreed it was important and that we would talk about it. But we haven't. I may bring it up again later. We could at least make simple lists—put something in writing. What would the list include?

What measures should be taken to prolong life?
Who should be there?
How should we gather friends and family?
What should final arrangements include?

What kind of memorial service would we want?
What should be done with possessions, art, and work?
How should we handle finances and responsibilities?
Should there be an ongoing memorial fund set up?

That's a pretty daunting list, huh? I never thought I'd be facing these issues at this time in my life. And I know that I'll want to talk to you about much of it.

I feel so tired. So depleted. That damn Desert Storm thunders on the other side of the world and Dan and I are mesmerized by all the TV coverage. We forcibly turn it off and escape into another chapter of *Tales of the City*.

Not just life but reality itself seems to be slipping away.

All for now. I'll see you this week.

Love,
Chris

Choosing to leave

Dear Tom,

    During our run last week, I told you I was planning to leave our men's support group. At our meeting the next Sunday, the group spent intimate moments unfolding my decision and their feelings about it. Though we had lost one member to AIDS two years before, this departure would be the first that the group could wrestle with while all parties were still present.

    There's a great Harold Arlen tune with lyrics by Truman Capote:

> Don't like good-byes, tears or sighs.
> I'm not too good at leaving time.
> I've got no taste for grieving time.
> Oh, no, no, no. Not me.

    I may not like good-byes, but too often in my life I've engineered them out of fear, confusion, or habit. There have been times when I've run away from love. And there have been times when I've turned away from friends, surrendering to my own flight response when I should have summoned courage and steadfastness.

    In leaving our men's group, I'm proud to say I engaged in none of these behaviors. In fact, I stayed longer than I might have just to be sure my reasons were of a higher order. My departure is AIDS-related, too. Dan's health has continued to deteriorate and more of my time is needed to support our home environment. The circle of friends who assist in our nurturing have become my new support group. I can no longer afford the luxury of affiliations that take me away from Dan, away from our home.

    Friendships with several of the guys in our group will continue to grow and deepen. I certainly need my friendship with you, Tom. More than ever and I know you will be there for me and for Dan.

Leaving the group is actually a collection of leavings—some more difficult than others—so I took the time during our last meeting to speak with each member of the group. In some cases, the good-byes carried a finality, the end of a comradeship. Other good-byes just marked a new direction for friendships that I know will endure.

The one-on-one conversations, each witnessed by the larger group of men, were remarkable in their balance of solemnity and poignancy. Soft voices. In recalling them I flash on that scene in westerns where the old frontier woman asks the lone-ranger character, "Where will you go, son?" But here, the concern and the nurturing were all among men.

Men can be so up front and yet so fathomless at the same time. Just one of the paradoxes we wrestle with in assembling our personae. I certainly have my share. Anyway, I'm glad I can talk this passage through with you. My handling the transition away from a loving environment, for *good* reasons, is a source of some pride for me. I feel a little less paradoxical. A little more genuine. More of a man.

Love,
Chris

"Take Time for a New God"

Dear Tom,

Can life be any more strained? Sinews pulled any tighter? I'm so aware of life's precarious balance, life's delicate tissues. Within and without. In my own life and my life with Dan. Life moves through irrevocable changes. Yet each day burns with such clear-minded purpose—to simply live.

Preparing for the concert with my friend Tim Grummon, I've tried to mold the rawness of my present experience into words and music. I want to tell you about one song in particular, "Take Time for a New God." I think I've written a personal, spiritual treatise, a declaration of religious yearnings and discovery. It begins quietly:

Take some time when you're angry
Take some time when you're sad
Take time for a new God
A boy needs a friend when he's feelin' bad.

Maybe just hanclapping with a bass line. And a deeper rhythm that foreshadows a building, driving strength. Gospel in feeling. Then the tempo levels, the accompaniment fills out, and I begin the verses.

Take time for a new God
One who listens to your dreams.
One who sits with the devil on your shoulder
One who knows you're so mad, you could scream.

Take time for a new God
Who helps you cry when you need to.
One who cradles your loved one so tender
One who knows that the caregiver bleeds too.

No magic words, no rigamarole
Gonna make God up, to suit my soul
It's all right 'cause creation's divine
And when I reach down inside, I'm gonna find
   the design.

That last quatrain feels percussive. Words blend with sounds
coming from great, moist depths.

Take some time for a new God.
One who listens to your prayers.
He's gonna listen, not because he's bowed to
He's gonna listen because he cares

Don't call him names, you won't see a face.
You just make your home a sacred place.
Know what you want and you might get what
you need
But don't think satisfaction's ever guaranteed

Take some time for a new God
One who listens to your dreams
One who sits with the devil on your shoulder
One who knows you're so mad
You could s-c-r-e-a-m-m-m-m-m-m.

The storm passes and relative calm prevails again.

Take some time when you're angry.
Take some time, when you're sad
Take time for a new God.
Make him the best friend you ever had.

In my spirituality, God and the devil must sit alongside each other. And alongside my aching, crowded head and heart. Dreams and prayers leaking out of every sense organ. I won't be abandoned at this time when every fiber stretches, every muscle braces against bone. Every thought, every feeling conspires in life's noblest exercise—survival.

Dan is so uncomfortable, so challenged. In the middle of the night, I wander the nocturnal stillness, walking up and down the sidewalk, humming a new melody, trying new words, crying old tears, and stopping to gaze unbelievably at all the darkened windows. Who's there? Who cares? Who can tell me what to do? Who can tell me what I'm feeling or even *how* to feel?

Tom, I've had to create my own God. He may not be a Christian God. And he is not a God I might have known as a child. My God is a forever new God, created a billion times over and over and over. He *must* care about me and family so I make him caring. My God *must* know about my dreams and prayers so I make him compassionate. God becomes the centerpiece of my world view, my vision for life and the living.

I want people to hear this song. I will nearly scream the last verse. I need someone to hear the ache of my heart, dear friend. I need God to cry with me.

I would think that the two forces in my life these days—tenderness and fury—would nearly paralyze me. Instead, they alternately propel me through the hours. In my writing and music I experience surprising agility and in friends and family I find a gratifying abundance of love. Creativity and sorrow till the same ground. Sacred ground where you and others, past and present, walk beside me. Thank you, friend.

Love,
Chris

Your beloved partner Dan dies

Dear Chris,

Your beloved partner and soul-mate, Daniel Stephen Lund, died at the age of thirty-seven. Partnerships are finally measured by depth not by length, and yours was body-and-soul deep.

Dan was the love of your life, and from my observations and your declarations, Chris, the most mutually satisfying partnership you have enjoyed. As you mentioned recently, "Dan and I were planning to get married!"

You stirred the spirits of one another as gifted artists: Dan as painter, you as singer. Your personalities complemented and stretched one another. During his protracted illness, you were a faithful caregiver, and Dan maintained spiritual equanimity and uncompromising hopefulness.

You were each blessed by the other's gifts and presence. Nothing will ever diminish or replace the power of your precious love.

The night of your concert with Tim Grummon, which featured the rare blending of vocalist and artist, held at our church, you turned, at the beginning of the performance, toward the hospital across the street where Dan lay dying of AIDS and you dedicated this night of creativity-and-compassion to your lover. I was seated next to your parents and our eyes clouded over with tears of sadness intermingled with gratitude and affection.

Near the end of the evening, the concert producer rushed down to the stage, whispered in your ear and you immediately raced off to the hospital to meet Dan's emergency need. We closed this beautiful, dramatic, agonizing concert by holding hands and singing the comforting hymn "Abide With Me."

For the remaining few days of Dan's life I regularly visited the two of you along with a stream of faithful friends and family. After holding you awhile, I would massage Dan's body, repeatedly offering this simple blessing of farewell:

Dan, you are loved.
Dan, you have loved.
Dan, your life is whole.
Dan, go now in peace to your eternal rest.

And when he was ready, he died, full of assurance and bathed in everlasting love.

Your friend,
Tom

Into the light

Dear Tom,

Thanks for making me a part of the service last Sunday. Six months after Dan's death, I was honored to share a tribute to him and to loving men everywhere with our church family. Now I'm putting that address into a letter to you, Tom, because I want to make it a part of our friendship chronicles.

> Tom asked me to join him today and speak about his new book, *Brother-Spirit,* and the publishing venture that has brought this attractive, important, and moderately priced book into all of our lives. I accepted the invitation.

I allowed myself to begin with some unabashed promotion. After all, we were both very proud of the book that you had written and I had edited and published.

> In keeping with Tom's *Brother-Spirit* theme, I want to share a personal story.

> Most of you know I'm a singer and it's in front of you, on this stage, that I've stretched that talent. When I sang for Tom's birthday last month, it was the first singing I'd done in quite a while. I never knew that music could drop out of my daily life like it did.

> In February last year, I stopped my early morning runs with Tom, largely because my lover Dan Lund, sick with a number of HIV-related conditions, needed more help at home and I knew my place was with him. I missed those early morning runs, Tom. I missed you, too. I missed a lot of you. But I did not miss the opportunity, the calling, to be with Dan, to be with Dan as no one else could.

> My contribution to this morning's message is one of testimony—a story of commitment between men—a personal commitment between two men that found expression in many ways—artistic, intellectual, emotional, and sexual. As most of you know, Dan died in the spring. AIDS took him away but, during our two years

together, AIDS did not come between us, it did not conquer us. It scrubbed us raw, made us achingly aware of our fragility, and it caused Dan terrible physical discomfort, but it did not conquer him. If anything it accelerated our deepening commitment to each other.

As an artist and as an educator, Dan's life was a continuous act of generosity—he was generous in spirit, in his art, in his humor, and in his love. Those of us who knew and loved him carry his gifts forward, each of us privileged to shoulder a unique slice of his legacy. My relationship with Dan is my life's proudest accomplishment to date. Enduring his loss challenges me, but I know his death was also his final healing . . . and that gives me some small comfort. I also draw comfort from memories of our time together, from his art that surrounds me at home, and from a four-line poem that appears on one of his monoprints:

> Beyond earthbound ties
> Into the light
> The onward journey
> Soul's infinite flight.

The love and support of friends like Tom and many of you breathe warmth and substance back into my life. I can tell you, it's working.

No project has been as important to me in that rebuilding as collaborating with Tom on his book, *Brother-Spirit*. Since that collaboration represents another type of commitment between men, I began to understand an important connection between my life with Dan and Tom's book. I wanted to strengthen that connection.

Taking Dan's ashes up to his boyhood home this summer, I was a little surprised and humbled to discover that Dan's spirit was already there—my pilgrimage just a tiny part of his journey home. His soul's infinite flight. "Bring him to us," the mountains seemed to say. Crowned with boiling clouds, they welcomed the dust that only earth can return to life. "He's home," the hills sang to each other, passing shadows and rainbows among themselves.

On August 3, a small tribe of people in Dan's life climbed up the pine-covered slopes of Bald Eagle Mountain in Northern Idaho to a rocky outcropping at the top and scattered Dan's ashes. That day forever lives in my heart.

I have chosen to call my new publishing venture Bald Eagle Mountain Press. I love the pairing of earth and sky in that name. How appropriate that our first book is named *Brother-Spirit*, a similar blend of counterpoised imagery. Bald Eagle Mountain Press is dedicated to stories of personal endeavor, growth, and revelation. Bald Eagle Mountain Press is dedicated to Dan and stands for the loving commitment between men and between people everywhere.

Tom, I'd like to close this letter, as I did that morning standing before my church family, with a reading from my journal:

I've seen differently since Dan died. The difference was especially strong in the first week or so. I was astonished by everyday sights—freeway on-ramps, plants, buildings, paintings. Another aspect of Dan's legacy. We do carry it on. Our task couldn't be more enriching or more precious. But like all gifts, it could be squandered, left undeveloped.

We build on each others' lives—like a colony of coral. The true inheritance between people. Those who would give—whether love, knowledge, instruction, art—and accept those gifts . . . they were all Dan's family.

Nature was Dan's great pleasure. What higher honor than to paint it as he saw and felt it? Pure intention, not unlike early hunters rendering sacred images of the day's kill on stone walls—those images leaping back at them in the smoky light. And what paints! Crushed stones and plants, blood and sweat. Paints giving form, form taking life, life returning to the endless wheel.

This breeze is so wonderful. These moments of rest so welcome. The wind lifts the pages of my journal and they ruffle, almost annoyingly; the noise of ten thousand words blending into a soft rattle—unintelligible.

Oh, my Danny Boy. What is this that grips us when we lose a loved one? What purpose does it serve? And am I true to that unfathomed purpose? And where are you in all this? Your absence is so ponderous. My ache so strong—both continual and relenting, like a cold water spring that travels alternately beneath a shining sun and then through the underground chambers of a hillside, with rocks and earth bearing silent witness. Where are you? In light or shadow?

I choose to believe what you told us—"into the light." Not surprising. As an artist, your life was a dance with light. Your eyes fed on it. And you taught us to do the same.

Hungry for light. That's how I understand my new eyes. They are hungry for light. As a musician, I've always catered to my ears' appetite. Thank you for the balance.

Sound and light. Earth and sky. An eagle soaring over a stately mountain. Brother–Spirit.

I love you forever.

And now I'll close my letter with a word of thanks: Thank you, Tom, for your gentle tugging and guiding and nudging during this time of grief. I know you too were influenced by Dan's gifts. Life for us will never be the same. But our lives are richer for having known him and, undeniably, our lives continue.

And so does our friendship. See you soon.

Love
Chris

Enduring

There is a land of the living and a land of the dead.
The bridge is love; the only truth, the only survival.

Thornton Wilder

As I said in my letter to Tom, "Life for us will never be the same." There is no shortage of other people's wisdom regarding the grieving process. And I have read and listened to and pondered some of this wisdom. But I learned early on that it was my *own* rhythms and feelings that needed the most attention. I learned to accept certain conditions—confusion, lack of energy, anxiety, prolonged sorrow and crying—as normal. And I tried not to escape any of them too quickly.

As individuals, we are given the best opportunity to learn balance when our footing is least secure, to learn perseverance when we are easily exhausted, to learn about celebration when we are in the middle of loss. I am still learning and the lessons come slowly. Nothing can be hurried.

After a few months I remember noticing that my own personal energy seemed to flow more freely again and that I sometimes felt constrained. I realized that I was ready to embody more than grief. I was ready to move with my life again. And I realized, my life had changed—my relationship with Dan, my stretching to meet challenges, and my grief had all served to transform me. And I would never leave any of them behind. They have become my new companions of love.

Later in the year, I met a wonderful man who had also lost his partner to AIDS and we have busily tended a growing relationship that feels very permanent and that enriches me in countless ways. I'm ever grateful for life's abundance.

This final set of letters finds Tom in familiar voice. I am initially introspective, even discombobulated, and then reclaim a certain feistiness in the final letter. Bouncing back? You bet! There's always more living, more projects, more crying, more singing, more grieving, more laughing . . . more *everything* to do!

And of course, more letters to write to my buddy Tom.

Machine plus friend equals happiness!

> As machines get to be more and more like people, people will come to be more and more like machines.

Joseph Krutch

Dear Chris,

I finally vanquished my obstinate computer-phobia and purchased an upgraded Macintosh Plus, complete with hard-drive and ten megabytes. It was *yours*, Chris, and you gave me first crack at buying it when you graduated to newer, more advanced equipment.

Now I can edit text with alacrity and produce clean copy more readily. The "Mac" hardly makes me a better writer, but it certainly makes me a more efficient one. They say gurus arrive when we are ready. Well, it took me until this last August to welcome into my household this mechanical wizard. Through my adult years I have progressed ever so slowly from manual to electric to electronic typewriters, always failing to enter the world of computers. Now I have crossed that threshold.

If total truth be told, Chris, there was one overriding reason for clenching this deal. It was *you*. Whenever I might languish in confusion or slip into insecurity, you have given me the green light to call for your assistance.

So, unquestionably the best thing about my new Mac is the friend that comes with it!

Your friend,
Tom

Valentine's Day Dance

Dear Chris,

There is no experience more stretching of my soul and senses than active participation in our "Everybody Can Dance With Anybody" Valentine's Day Dances the last few years at the church. Gays, lesbians, bisexuals and straights are all invited. Couples and singles are included. Children accompanied by adults come, so do teenagers. Persons from the larger San Diego community hear the word and show up as well.

While growth-producing, the dance isn't a uniformly smooth experience for any of us. Me included. Especially close encounters with other men. There was the time when a gay man from the non-Church community, unknown to me, tried to "put the make" on me, assuming I was gay, and I clumsily turned down his offer to dance. It's doubly awkward when you're the welcoming, host minister who has to reject unwanted advances from an outsider. I wasn't taught how to negotiate that challenge in my seminary training.

There are other concerns. I am far more comfortable dancing a fast than a slow dance with another man. Furthermore, being a high-control individual, it is less difficult for me to ask, than to be asked to dance, by a man. When I take the lead, I know my intentions. I pretty much dictate the flow. When I am pursued, things get muddled: which of the two of us men will lead this dance? How will our bodies hold one another and where? A brief, basic embrace with a man is okay by me, but a sustained one can cause me to wiggle nervously. I also dance more easily with a straight than a gay man, because of the essentially flat erotic energy conveyed, and gambol most awkwardly with a bisexual man because of the confusing signals.

Our non-sexist dances always remind me that I have ample anxiety-buttons intact which are pushed when relating closely or physically with other men. I gain more confidence year after year, but some insecurities are ineradicable, a condition which remains understandable and fine with me. I am not interested in pushing the river. I want to flow with it.

It is imperative that I clarify my comfort levels in negotiating physical proximity with another man. I believe it is possible to maintain unleaky boundaries while not constructing walls. I can set my limits and respect those of another man, even as we risk closer fondness.

Each year, as the evening evolves, our Valentine's Day dance finds few people pairing off, and most of us swirling in clusters, as circle dancers, an amazing array of ages and affectional desires. A rare and holy form of communion.

As Emma Goldman, the great social activist, was reported to have said, "I never want to be a part of any revolution where there isn't dancing." So, each year, on Valentine's Day, for a few hours, our revolution *is* dancing.

Your friend,
Tom

Non-linear

Dear Tom,

As I'm writing dates these days—always at the top of every page, upper left corner—I pause momentarily before writing the year. The pen hovers and my mind spins like a roulette wheel. The ball falls into the slot, I mutter, "Of course," and I write the date. An observer might not even detect the pause but I live out a drama in my head as my hand rests, poised above the paper for that brief instant.

It's not like the confusion one endures in early January, writing last year on this year's checks. The confusion is bigger, grander. The roulette wheel seems to have all years represented: '49, '63, '71, '78, '81 . . . "Ah, '91! Of course!" The ball finds a slot and the wheel spins down to a stop. If the ball had slipped into another slot, would I loop back in time and shift gears to recreate my life as it was in, say, 1978? Am I trying to fit the pieces together? See the connections? Are the dates on the wheel in chronological sequence? Do some have more than one slot?

Would I really trade today for one of the others? What's behind the image of my life spinning, fragmented, and overlaid with this illusion of randomness, this game of chance?

I've concluded that my life isn't linear anymore. Never mind that I'll write the "correct" date at the top of each page until the next year comes. Or that I still skip a line between paragraphs or any of my other little writing conventions. I feel my life—in all of its perceived fragments, years, events—present now.

The moment can become so impossibly crowded that things freeze. Life implodes, the music stops, and the pen lifts from the page. One has the sense that any one thing written is a lie because it can not possibly communicate the whole truth.

The writer communicates truth one "lie" at a time, if you will. The pen glides along an infinite number of points; the artist's brush makes a single yet ever changing connection with the canvas. The singular point of expressive activity belies the multiplicity that drives it. A reservoir of feelings and experience strains against the earthen dam from which a single stream of water flows—feeble by comparison.

I have to laugh. I have a tendency to tackle big subjects and then get overwhelmed by them, freeze up, and wrap things up much too simply. I often finish my writings just as I reach the bottom of the page. The multiplicity can be petrifying—like the snakes on Medusa's head. "Behold. I give you truth. But first, assume the nature of stone for eternity." Ah, the myths really tell it like it is, huh? Sometimes, you have to get the right twist on it, but sometimes I think it's all there—on someone else's page. Anyway, truth hides in a tangle of lies because lies comprise our language. Question marks go everywhere here. No facts. No pronouncements. No intended arrogance.

Just trying to find my way. Just trying to keep the pen moving across that endless multitude of points. My journey . . . at least to the bottom of the page.

Love,
Chris

Being queer

> What makes heterosexuality work is heterosexual privilege—and if you don't have a sense of what privilege is, I suggest that you go home and announce to everybody that you know—a roommate, your family, the people you work with—everywhere that you go, that you're a queer. Try being a queer for a week.

Charlotte Bunch

Dear Chris,

As a concerned compatriot in the vineyards for gay rights and justice, there are times when I must break my silence and speak out against the heinous, despicable crimes specifically targeted against gays, lesbians, and bisexuals—my friends, including you.

The contemporary American myth is that the gay and lesbian community is homefree in modern times. The assumption is that oppression has diminished and a powerful minority of vocal people is flexing its political muscle. The reality is that gay-bashing and hate-mongering are as prevalent as ever, even among some of today's so-called enlightened youth. Anti-gay routines are common in the media and the AIDS crisis is used by bigots to engender religious discrimination and justify civil prejudice.

It remains imperative for straights like myself to show unflagging solidarity with our gay brothers and lesbian sisters. We need to emerge from our safe and secure hiding places of privilege and power. We need to combat, with all available personal and political resources, the homophobia and heterosexism that contaminate American society.

The battle rages fiercely for justice and dignity, and there is no time to lose. This is no era to wallow in neutrality, spectating from the sidelines. Rather it is time for supportive fellow-travelers to break silence and engage in resistance. But we can't speak out until we first abandon our comfortable closets. When Thucydides was asked if justice would come to Athens, the Greek philosopher replied, "Justice will not come to Athens until those who are not injured are as indignant as those who are injured." Now there was a historian who was also a card-carrying agent of social change!

Being a practicing heterosexual means never being lambasted with the label "queer." I didn't earn such freedom from denigration. It is simply my undeserved status, by dint of heterosexist privilege. I want to share with you the dictionary entry for "queer."

> Queer: eccentric, unconventional, strange, questionable, suspicious, touched, mildly insane, sexually deviate . . .
>
> Webster's Dictionary

Because of my religious convictions and political actions, I am unswervingly gay-affirmative and lesbian-supportive. This means I would be willing to be identified as gay in certain contexts to display solidarity with my gay brothers. As such, I reside clearly outside the mainstream of American opinion and behavior. Yet, however unorthodox and occasionally radical my attitudes may be, I will never be scorned outright as a queer. I will never be the target of that socially irredeemable term. Note that the further one travels along Webster's definitions, the more degrading the words get.

Actually, upon deeper reflection, Chris, I have been singed a bit in my history by the fires of hostility and discrimination. Seldom directly, most often by association. When I marched arm-in-arm with blacks in Selma, Alabama in 1965, I was cursed as a "nigger-lover." Our car has been slammed because we support therapeutic abortions. Our church, for its unequivocal, relentless advocacy of gay and lesbian rights, identity, and services of union, has been a locus of "queer-bashing" over the years.

I loathe the term "queer." For, Chris, there is nothing queer about homosexuality, nothing queer about you, nothing queer about straights like myself standing up for variant lifestyles, nothing queer about our friendship.

Unusual, perhaps, but nothing queer.

Your friend,
Tom

Why not *"Queer"?*

Dear Tom,

Thanks for the note. I do feel your strong support and your genuine willingness to identify with gays and lesbians as we fight for our civil rights. Our cause is strengthened when we march arm-in-arm with our non-gay friends. When an issue of human rights is on the line, there can be no outsiders. I'm reminded of our band of church goers—straights, gays, and kids—marching in the annual Gay Pride parades. Can you hear us? "Hey, hey! Ho, ho! Homophobia's got to go!" It always brings lots of cheers and applause from the people lining the parade route.

I appreciate your concern about the bursts of verbal and physical violence that gay men and lesbians deal with, sometimes on a daily basis. Hate seems as strong a motivator as love when it comes to human expression. The variety of expressions extruded from twisted lips and maniacal eyes staggers the heart and leaves us numb. That's the difference between love and hate. Hate destroys, hate empties, hate negates. There's nothing there to hold on to and grow with. And the expression spawned by hate deforms us, scars us, disheartens us.

It's no wonder that throughout history we humans have had to continually re-inscribe golden rules, commandments, bills of rights, and assorted fundamentals for living on nearly every available surface—loving behavior does not seem to arise automatically from our internal circuitry. Goodness battles for air during a treacherous ascent to the surface of our human consciousness. And yet the practice of goodness remains a heart-felt aspiration for most of us.

Growing up, I guess I absorbed at least my share of verbal salvos consisting of "faggot," "homo," and "queer." And I'm sure there were times when I even hurled the same words right back. Or maybe I absorbed them just long enough to squeeze them back out onto some poor soul, a little lower on the playground pecking order. These epithets and many more like them are weapons—sharp instruments meant to inflict damage. "Sticks and stones," I sometimes defended myself, "may break my bones, but words will never hurt me." I can't say I ever experienced great comfort in that adage but I loved the idea. "Faggot" and "queer" may be just words (or unjust words)—powerful, symbolic, black-on-white, dangerous, ugly words—but their weight grows as a function of the numbers of people who use them as weapons. A hateful tone of voice sharpens the point, the point is smeared with poison by a curled lip. And there may be a counter blow dealt from the inside when you realize these awful words might actually reveal a dreaded reality, might describe your destiny, might explain all those things you have been noticing about yourself.

Words are weapons and weapons hurt. But can we turn the words around? Unhitch them from their hostile associations, or better yet, make their impact boomerang and stun the provoker? You might not know about a new activist group of largely young gay men and lesbians who proudly call themselves "Queer Nation." Yes, Tom, there is a growing number of gay men and lesbians who are embracing the label "queer." And did you know that among ourselves we toss "faggot" and "dyke" back and forth with an ease that would astound you. Why? Because we need to disarm these words. Transform them from weapons back to words. Words with new meanings. Words that connote "pride," "uniqueness," even "strangeness" and "eccentricity."

As you pointed out, the further down the list of Webster's definitions for "queer," the more derogatory the meaning. We're just working our way back to the top of the list.

Reclaiming these words can help neutralize the verbal artillery out there. Oh, yeah, the hate still comes through but wearing a "queer" badge proudly can also confuse and frustrate the hate-mongers. I don't pretend to know all about Queer Nation. I'm not a member and have never been to a meeting. They have made all of us in the gay and lesbian community aware of a yawning generation gap within our ranks. But it's good to be reminded of our diversity. So much variation among us.

All this semantics . . .

Tom, I wonder how you feel about "straight" as a descriptor? Or try this one—"breeders." Stings a little, huh? That's how gays sometimes refer to (procreating) heterosexuals. It still brings a chuckle out of me when I hear it. But I wouldn't be amused if I heard hatred in the tone of voice. Though maybe I've overlooked a couple of times when there was. Hate can be so seductive in its disguises.

As a writer, I rely on the power of words, I respect the integrity of language. I also resist any system of rigid conventions and language sometimes fits that description. We need the power to loosen that which binds us. We need to reclaim words that have been used as weapons. We need words we can sing out with a heart filled with love not hate.

Incidentally, I agree that our friendship isn't queer. But I'd be interested to learn why you think it's unusual.

Really? Unusual? Let's just agree it's special.

Love,
Chris

 # Epilog

Ob-La-Di, Ob-La-Da

Dear Reader,

CHRIS:

Not to be flippant about life's passages but I've always loved the Beatles' song, "Ob–La–Di, Ob–La–Da" as a cheerful, not–too–serious expression of life's capacity for joy and fulfillment. A jaunty tune with a bouncy, head–nodding chorus:

> Ob-La-Di, Ob-La-Da
> Life goes on, bra
> La, La, how the life goes on!

Dan and so many friends have died and yet so many of us live on. In the months after losing Dan I would repeat to myself and to others a simple explanation, "I have more to do in this life." My life still unfolds and I thank God for the strength and the desire to pursue its course. With a wonderful new partner, new projects, more singing, and bountiful friendships gracing my life, horizons refuse to rest against the sky, so they stretch beyond.

Tom and I have temporarily fallen out of our weekly running schedule but we see each other often and delight in each other's company.

TOM:

And my life is shifting as well. Two of our children got married in the last year. Of the remaining two—one moved away to be on his own in Northern California and our youngest is slowly winding her way through the rigors of the collegiate maze.

My friendship with Chris faced its first potential jolt since we met back in 1981 as Carolyn and I nearly left San Diego to sink fresh roots in Boston. That opportunity has now passed so Chris and I continue to be spoiled by being able to see one another up close whenever we want.

CHRIS and TOM:

Whether the future finds us side by side or separated by great distance, our friendship endures, blessing both of our lives with ineffable riches.

Michelangelo portrayed the gift of life with the almost touching hands of God and Adam on the ceiling of the Sistine Chapel. For us, the touch between human and human rises above all other gifts. For those of us with good friends, how could we believe otherwise?

Love,
Chris and Tom

Mail order information:

For additional copies of **Friendship Chronicles,** send $12.95 plus $2.00 per book for shipping and handling (add 7% sales tax in California). Make checks payable to Bald Eagle Mountain Press and mail to the publisher: Bald Eagle Mountain Press, 9985 Huennekens St., Suite B, San Diego, CA 92121.

For information on other books by Tom Owen-Towle, write to the author at 3303 Second Avenue, San Diego, CA 92103.